F●ck You I'm Italian

⇥ *Why We Italians Are Awesome* ⇤

Tony DiGerolamo

Published by:
Ulysses Press
P.O. Box 3440
Berkeley, CA 94703
www.ulyssespress.com

ISBN: 978-1-61243-782-8 (hardback)
ISBN: 978-1-64604-347-7 (paperback
Library of Congress Control Number: 2018930786

Printed in the United States

10 9 8 7 6 5 4 3 2 1

Acquisitions editor: Casie Vogel
Managing editor: Claire Chun
Editor: Shayna Keyles
Proofreader: Renee Rutledge
Production: Caety Klingman
Cover design: what!design @ whatweb.com
Cover images from shutterstock.com: pizza © La puma; wine ©
    bioraven; Colosseum © doom.ko; retro singer © berdsigns
Interior images from shutterstock.com: chapter title graphics © Fine
    Art Studio; folio and subhead graphics © Svetlana Kononova

To my dad,
who taught me everything about being Italian.

Contents

Introduction 7

1. The Roman Empire and Italy:
   When Italians Ran Things. 12

2. Italy: Where the Best Food in the World Is . . . 31

3. America Wasn't Cool Until the
   Italians Came. 57

4. Family: The Only People That Put Up
   with Your Shit 70

5. There Is No Mafia (But If There Were,
   Here's What We'd Know). 80

6. Teaching Medigans 98

7. Our Major Holidays 112

8. Gambling and Other Italian Religious
   Practices 125

9. Sinatra and Other Famous Italians. 130

10. Famous Italians You Didn't Know
Were Italian 151

11. Talk Like a Paisan: A Handy Glossario
of Italian Words. 160

12. Great Moments in Italian History. 166

About the Author. 192

Introduction

Hey, you. Yeah, you. You were smart to buy this book, and you're probably one of the best-looking people to buy it. Seriously, I wouldn't blow smoke up your ass.

This book is about Italians and Italian culture, and why it's the best. If you're not Italian, this book will be an invaluable tool so you don't look like a *gavone* in front of your Italian friends. And if you are Italian, you already know we're the best. And who don't like to confirm good news, am I right?

....

gavone. 1) clod, lower class. 2) a glutton, a pig.

My brother-in-law went right to the appetizer table at the wedding and stuffed his fat face like the gavone he is!

....

I don't mean to brag, but there's more to Italians than pasta and the *Godfather* movies. (The first two. We don't talk about the third one.) The Roman Empire conquered the world and, believe me, the guys running that show liked their *scungilli* and sauce.

....

scungilli. an Italian dish featuring sliced conch.

This scungilli tastes a little fishy, I hope it was fresh.
....

Italians shaped history, invented things, and contributed a lot to the culture of the world. I mean, a whole lot. And no, it wasn't through Mafia connections, because the Mafia don't exist. That's only in the movies. But if it did exist, we got a big chapter about what we'd know if it did. *Capeche?* And not only that, we're going to be talking about traditions, family, and food. You can't be Italian and skip the food. It's just a rule.

....

capeche. Italian for "Understand?"

You gotta hold a pizza box level or the cheese will slide all over. Capeche?
....

So sit back and enjoy the ride because you're about to learn everything about Italians, plus several good recipes for spaghetti sauce so you never have to have it from a jar like a *Medigan* again.

....

Medigan. Italian immigrants' bad pronunciation of "American"; it means any non-Italian.

You're dating a Medigan? Who is going to cook for you?
....

And if you are Italian, you're probably already saying, "F*ck you, I'm Italian!" Just read the book, *stunad*. You don't want any gaps in your Italian knowledge.

....

stunad. a dumb person, a moron.

Hey, stunad! Don't splash that red sauce on my track suit!
....

Italian Culture and Perceptions

Before we go any further, let's get something out of the way. Overall, Italian culture can be broken down into basic components: family, food, and tradition, lots of which you'll read about soon. Just know that you don't mess with an Italian's family, you must have respect for our traditions, and don't ever, God forbid, bring us to an Olive Garden. That's where Medigans who don't know Italian food go to eat.

Positive Perceptions

Most people will tell you that Italians have great hair, are confident and attractive, know how to eat, know how to cook, are awesome singers, and are friends with everybody. Too true.

Negative Perceptions

1. We're all loud: Not true. We got plenty of quiet Italians. They're just smart enough not to talk to you. It's just that the loud Italians are very loud. See? We're good at both, being quiet and loud.

2. We're all in the Mafia: False. There ain't no Mafia, so how could we be in something that don't exist?

3. We're greasy: We are not. That is a leftover stereotype from the '50s greasers, many of whom were Italian and very cool.

4. We talk with our hands: No. We are excited to be talking and tend to show our excitement with our hands. Big difference.

5. We all love Frank Sinatra music: Not true. Everyone likes Frank Sinatra music, not just Italians.

CHAPTER ONE

The Roman Empire and Italy: When Italians Ran Things

Romulus and Remus

No one was actually witness to these two Italian brothers establishing Rome, but we pieced together what we think might've happened. Ya see, like any good Italians, Romulus and Remus were good at giving directions to people. But back then, there weren't too many roads. You had to tell people to turn at this rock or that tree or whatever. Then you'd confuse the second tree with the first rock! No one could get anywhere, no matter how good the directions were. Then the brothers had an idea.

ROMULUS: Where the fuck have you been? I've been waitin' an hour!

REMUS: Oh! You kiss our mother with that mouth?

ROMULUS: Mom's a wolf, Remus. I don't kiss her at all. She'd bite my lips off.

REMUS: Oh, right.

ROMULUS: So why were you late?

REMUS: These friggin' Trojans asked me for directions. Took all day to tell 'em!

ROMULUS: You told them to follow the beach along that rock, right?

REMUS: Of course! You save like 10 minutes goin' that way! But they got the rocks confused.

ROMULUS: Well, they're not from around here...

REMUS: Exactly! That's when I got to thinkin', what if we built a place where all roads lead? We'll call it Rome, and that way, we can give directions!

ROMULUS: Won't they get the roads confused?

REMUS: No, we give the roads different names, stunad!

ROMULUS: Don't call me a stunad, I don't like it. But I like your idea. I'm in!

And thus, Rome was born around 753 BC. Romulus killed his brother and became the first king of Rome. He didn't like to be called a stunad.

Rome: The Early Days

Before the Romans came onto the scene, there were these guys called the Etruscans in the Tuscany region. "Etruscan" is where Tuscany gets its name. The Etruscans were mainly farmers, and they also made wine. They didn't have no red sauce or roads to help give people directions, although they probably had decent bread. These guys lasted from about 700 BC to 350 BC, until the Romans took over.

The Romans had kings for a couple hundred years until some douchebag named Lucius Tarquinius Superbus screwed it all up in 509 BC. Lucius's son raped the wife of a nobleman and she committed suicide. Needless to say, this didn't sit well with the rank and file. Lucius thought he'd sweep it under the rug because he was king, but Italians don't let dishonor go unavenged. The king got deposed, and Rome became a republic. From then on, Rome was ruled by two consuls and a senate. It was like having two co-presidents and half of Congress, just talkin' it out.

In 450 BC, the first Roman code of law was inscribed on 12 bronze tablets in the Forum. The Forum was like the White House, the Supreme Court, a mall, and a football stadium all rolled into one. Mainly, it was a place where politicians argued over laws and policies. (I'm sure one of the senators had a cousin or a brother that did some nice marble work around there.) The code listed things like civil rights and property rights.

Things were lookin' pretty good until 390 BC, when the Gauls sacked Rome. That's when the Romans knew the Gauls had to go. Rome struck back and took the whole Italian boot by 264 BC. These were good times. Italians were everywhere, even though they weren't called Italians yet. There still weren't things called pizza or pasta, but we always had good bread, so this was a major plus to the people that got conquered. And all the new roads meant that you could get bread in a timely manner.

Cement

Speaking of roads, one of the greatest contributions to the world from the Italians of Rome was cement. We learned to mix it with volcanic ash so it wouldn't crack so much. Why do you think so many buildings from Rome are still standing today, huh? We don't mess around when it comes to construction.

Marcus Vitruvius Pollio was a first-century *goomba* that wrote it all down in his book *De architectura*. He said, "Proportion is that agreeable harmony between the several parts of a building, which is the result of a just and regular agreement of them with each other; the height to the width, this to the length, and each of these to the whole." That's friggin' poetry about construction! Nothing more Italian than that.

....

goomba. fellow countryman, fellow Italian, friend, comrade, etc.

Hey, goomba. Take this twenty and maybe give me a table near the window, huh?

....

The Greeks

We always liked the Greeks. That's why the Romans conquered them in 146 BC. Instantly, we adopted a lot of their style. Their gods, their literature, their art—hey, we liked it all. I mean, your average Greek restaurant is basically an Italian restaurant with less sauce and more feta cheese and olives. And as far as civilizations go, the Greeks had lots of stuff worked out, so it's not like we wanted to reinvent the wheel. Sure, they break plates once in a while and they got that weird fisherman's hat, but they're all right.

Julius Caesar

Julius Caesar was like the Sylvester Stallone of the Romans. You couldn't keep this guy down! (Well, except the last time.) Julius was the master of Roman politics. He was a member of the First Triumvirate in 59 BC, which was basically just him and the also-rans. Then he left Rome, kicked the asses of all the Gauls in 55 BC, and then brought his army back to Italy by crossing the Rubicon River on January 10, 49 BC. This was technically illegal in Rome, and it's where the expression "crossing the Rubicon" comes from. It means you just stepped into some deep shit!

And like at the end of *Godfather II*, Caesar took out all his enemies in a short time. As the boss, he ran

Rome as a dictator in July of 48 BC, but other families—other Romans—weren't too happy about that. Although Caesar instituted some really good economic reforms, improved the calendar, created all sorts of construction projects, and busted up some of the monopolies held by the senators of Rome, the other powerful Romans didn't like the idea of losing money in their side businesses, even though it made them corrupt. And they really didn't like the idea of an emperor.

Some say Julius pushed things too far. There is actually a theory that Caesar, who suffered from epilepsy, orchestrated his own assassination! (This happened on the Ides of March, March 15th, in 44 BC.) Rumor has it that as his epilepsy was getting worse, he wanted to die like a real Roman: proud, dignified, not curled up in a ball suffering from muscle spasms. (Keep in mind, although Rome was pretty advanced, they couldn't cure that.) Julius had already chosen Octavian as his successor—he left him the majority of his vast fortune and still had enough left over to give every single citizen in Rome 75 drachmas. That's around $200 today. So imagine the president dropping dead and leaving every citizen two Benjamins. That's a pretty generous dead guy!

But even with all that money given away, plus funding a giant park in the middle of Rome, Octavian was still the richest guy in Rome, and in the world. Julius made Donald Trump look like a Salvation Army Santa by comparison. Like his mentor, Octavian was a genius when it came to Roman politics and military strategy. Julius knew that. Badda boom, badda bing, Octavian took over, changed his name to Augustus, and became the first Emperor of Rome.

The Roman Empire

When the Romans ran the world, they really ran it! There were roads going everywhere, coliseums so people could watch the game, and Madonn', the food! You couldn't throw a stick without finding a good place. No one even knew what it was like to sit down at a table that didn't have at least a bottle of olive oil, some red wine, and good bread. It was like one 200-year-long Saint Gennaro Festival that never ended, only there were more swords.

....

Madonn'. an expression of surprise, like "holy shit!"; short for "the Madonna."

Madonn'! Look at that chick! She's incredible!
....

Emperors, however, were still family. And not everyone was exactly good at running the family business. Guys like Caligula and Nero did some messed up stuff.

Caligula became emperor in 37 AD. He banged his sisters and even turned the palace into a brothel. Talk about your uncomfortable Sunday dinners! They say he once got bored at the Coliseum during intermission and had his soldiers throw members of the audience to the lions—now there's a halftime show. Probably the dumbest thing he did was when he tried to appoint his horse to political office. When that didn't work, he made him a priest!

Nero was kind of the Norman Bates of Roman emperors. He was only 16 when he was made emperor in 54 AD. His mother pulled the strings. Unfortunately for her, she tugged a little too hard. First Nero banned her from the palace, and then he had her killed in 59 AD. This sent Nero into a downward spiral. Then, when one of his top advisors died in 62 AD, he cracked. Totally paranoid and *oobatz*, he started holding trials for treason. In July of 64 AD, he really freaked out and set the entire city of Rome on fire. By 68 AD, people had had enough of his bullshit. Before soldiers could come and beat him to death, he stabbed himself and said, "Oh, what an artist dies in me."

....

oobatz. crazy.

You want to go to the beach in October? That's oobatz!

....

Rome bounced back with some new blood, but after Commodus took over in 180 AD, well, let's just say you wished Russell Crowe had survived that mook in *Gladiator*. Commodus was so stupid, his own advisors had to strangle him in the bath.

During the 200s, there were so many emperors getting whacked, you would have needed a score card to keep track of them, if score cards had been invented yet. A lot of the whackin' was done by the Praetorian Guard. They were like the Secret Service, if the Secret Service suddenly started whackin' and then picking the president.

....

whacked. to be murdered.

When Lee Harvey Oswald whacked JFK, there was a lot of controversy.

....

By the 300s, things were in decline, but Rome was still holding together.

Christianity: The Catholic Church Arrives

In 324 AD, Emperor Constantine converted to Christianity, and all the Romans converted with him. Immediately, no one could do shit on Sundays but go to church and have Sunday dinner with the family. Fortunately, the dinner was super early, so you could still catch a late game at the Coliseum.

Constantine ordered religious freedom throughout the empire, but in 380 AD, Emperor Theodosius put a stop to that and declared Christianity the state religion. (Probably because he had a weird name. What do you call a buddy with that name? Theo, I guess. Not exactly a terrifying emperor name. "Look out! Emperor Theo's armies are attacking!" It don't quite work. He probably had a complex.)

Anyhow, that meant everybody had to go to mass, confess to the priest, and not look cross-eyed at a nun, or *whack!*

The Fall of Rome

Rome wasn't built in a day, and it sure as hell took a long time to fall apart, too. After centuries of Rome running the world, the world decided it would take turns running Rome. During the Middle Ages it was taken over by the Ostrogoths; the Byzantines; the Lombards, the Franks, and other Germanic tribes: the Moors; Spain; and on and on. Italians, who weren't called Italian yet, were thinking that maybe building all those roads so that people could get around quickly wasn't such a great idea after all.

By the 14th century, Italy was mostly a bunch of city-states battling it out on the peninsula. Venice, Florence, Pisa, Genoa—these weren't just places to get your blinds and salami. They were actual political powers and almost countries in their own right. It was kinda like if New York, Chicago, LA, and Philadelphia were all in Florida, constantly fighting with each other and Miami.

The next thing you know, the Renaissance starts. One minute, every goomba in a 200-mile radius is trying to kill each other, and the next year they're painting and sculpting to beat the band. Go figure. Guess we got all that fighting out of our system.

The Renaissance

The Renaissance, which lasted from around 1300 to 1500, was considered one of the greatest eras of literature, art, and culture for mankind. No surprise that it was all the idea of the Italians. After years of everyone banging their heads together and living in the mud, the Italians were finally like, "Ho! Listen up! No more dickin' around, let's get some civilization goin' here!"

In places like Florence and Venice, rich guys paid scholars, philosophers, and artists to basically live like college students. It was a movement called humanism. Rich guys like the Medicis were patrons to people like Leonardo da Vinci and Galileo.

Without da Vinci, you wouldn't have the *Mona Lisa*, his work on human anatomy, or his plans for flying machines and submarines, all before anyone could build them. And don't forget the other guys named after ninja turtles: Raphael, Donatello, and

Michelangelo—they were all Italian masters of art from that time.

Galileo dropped two different-sized cannonballs off the Leaning Tower of Pisa, proving all objects fall at the same rate of acceleration. But he also proved that the Earth and other planets revolve around the sun, not the other way around. The very powerful Catholic Church had him locked up, but he never recanted, which means the biggest balls that guy had were in his pants! Oh!

Modern Italy

Italy wasn't actually Italy until 1861. That's why we're such a fiercely independent people. Even Italians are independent from each other! You Sicilian? You from Napoli? These things matter!

The whole thing started around 1829. A bunch of little duchies were unified over the years after Napoleon finally crapped out on the battlefield. The Carbonari were very active during this time. They were like Italian Freemasons, dedicated to the cause of a unified Italy. By 1859, Parma, the duchies, and Florence were basically all unified under the United Provinces of Central Italy. (The whole thing is way more complicated than that. You could literally write whole books on this, but just imagine a few dozen Italians that have their own armies in an argument, and that they keep arguing for decades.)

Then the Kingdom of Sardinia moved in. Sardinia wasn't just the island then. It also controlled a big hunk of northern Italy. Count Camillo Benso di Cavour was very big in the Sardinian government in 1852, and he was all about helping Victor Emmanuel II (the King of Sardinia) unite the Italians. By 1860, Florence joined the Kingdom of Sardinia.

The south was called the Kingdom of the Two Sicilies. One was the Sicily that exists today, and the other was everything south of what were then the Papal States. Francis II was the last king before Sardinia conquered the area.

The last holdouts were the Papal States. Although Italy was declared a nation in 1861, the Papal States and the Kingdom of Venetia were still on their own. The capital of Italy was Florence until finally, in 1866, Venetia came in, and the Papal States followed in 1870. The Pope actually had his own army back then, if you can believe it. This was a huge success for Italy. Imagine Italy with no Rome and no Pope. It would be like imagining a pizza with no crust, or Frankie Valli without the Four Seasons!

The whole country was unified under a king, including the boot and the islands, but we were late to the game. You see, by then, kingdoms weren't exactly in style, and after World War I, things kinda fell apart. Italians can't stop inventing things, and we invented fascism. Benito Mussolini came to power. The Italians were forced to call him Il Duce (or, as I like to say, Il Douchebag), which meant "The Leader."

Fortunately, by World War II, plenty of Italians lived in the States, so the Americans, grateful for the advancements in pasta and sauce, helped us kick Mussolini's ass. He was met with an unfortunate "accident," courtesy of some friends of ours, and we hung his fat ass from a gas station roof. Fuck that guy.

The upshot was that after the war, Italy became a republic and remains one to this day. Italy became a member of NATO, invented Vespas, and now it has Starbucks and iPhones and all the modern conveniences.

Not to mention some of the best food in the world!

....

Vespa. brand of Italian scooter popular in Italy; the word means "wasp" in Italian.

I rode my Vespa to get some espresso. Fortunately, none of my friends saw me.

....

CHAPTER TWO

Italy: Where the Best Food in the World Is

You'd better get yourself a sandwich or something for this chapter, because it's all gonna be about food. And if you're not hungry reading about this stuff, then you must be some kind of soulless robot that don't eat nothin'.

So We Didn't Technically Invent Pasta

But we perfected it. We would've eventually gotten around to inventing it. But hey, we can't invent everything!

During the time of Augustus, in the first century, the Roman poet Horace mentions *lagana*. Lagana is made of sheets of fried dough with layers of meat. Sound familiar? Yeah, this was probably the early version of lasagna, but since no one has a time machine, we'll just have to guess.

Now, a lot of you may think that Marco Polo brought the recipes for noodles back from China. He did, but he compared them to lasagna. So if you had lasagna, you already had pasta, stupid! This urban legend may have gained popularity because in 1929, the National Pasta Association pushed the story in their trade magazine to promote pasta.

Turns out, when the Moors took over Sicily in the 5th century, over 500 years before Marco Polo, they already had dried pasta that you could boil in water. Pasta as we know it became popular during the Renaissance, but here's the weird thing—they didn't have no sauce! Can you imagine? I hope butter wasn't invented yet, because I would hate to think Italians were eatin' pasta like a bunch of Medigans!

The first mention of sauce comes in a 1790 book written by the great Italian chef, Francesco Leonardi, called *L'Apicio moderno*. No offense to Francesco, but I think we can all assume he got the sauce recipe from somebody's grandmother who used to make it every Sunday.

Today, Italy has around 350 types of pasta. You got your fresh and your dried pasta. There's nothing like the fresh stuff, and it takes half as long to cook, too. Still, you gotta have some dried stuff on hand, 'cause you can store it forever. Some of these pastas are known by different names according to the time period, the shape, and the area of Italy where they originated.

The broad categories are long pastas, short pastas, ribbon-cut, miniatures, pasta with filling, and the weird or decorative cuts. Remember Fusilli Jerry on *Seinfeld*? Fusilli is one of my personal favorites, 'cause it's the corkscrew-looking pasta. It holds the sauce real good. Most decent Italian restaurants will have fusilli, spaghetti, fettuccine, angel hair, rigatoni, linguine, lasagne (for the lasagna), penne, gnocchi, orzo, ravioli, tortellini, bow tie, shells, ziti, and man-icotti. I mean, if you don't have the basics, you might as well close shop, right?

Now for some of the shapes you don't see as often. These include *lumaconi*, which look like little snail shells. *Fiori* is a pasta that kinda looks like honeycomb cereal pieces. You also got *croxetti*, which are flat, coin-shaped, and sometimes stamped with a symbol or coat of arms. *Calamarata* is pasta that looks like calamari pieces, so it's probably more than a coinci-dence that their names are similar. There's also *bigoli*, which looks like thick spaghetti with a hole running through it. It's like you're eatin' the cable TV wire. *Radiatori* pieces look like little radiators. And finally, you got pastas like *grattini* that look like little pieces of irregularly shaped grain. Ya know, if you decide the pieces of orzo were too big for you.

There are literally hundreds more, but we gotta move on.

Pizza: That Thing Everyone Likes

Where did pizza come from? Depends on what you call pizza. And if you call that Chicago deep-dish stuff pizza, then you'll pretty much call anything pizza. Pizza scientists agree that Neolithic people were making flatbread on a stone over a fire, which is kinda like how pizza today is made. Then one of the guys would carry it to the cave that ordered it, get his tip, and go back to the fire to make another.

Other cultures had the same type of thing. Persian soldiers used to eat flatbread with cheese that they cooked on their shields in the 6th century. The Romans in the 1st century had flatbread with olive oil, herbs, and honey. But that ain't pizza! You think Papa John's is going to bring you that?

The word "pizza" first appeared in 997 AD in Gaeta, Italy. The church records said that the bishop was to receive 12 pizzas on Christmas Day. There must've been some tip for the driver. Pizza was mostly a central/southern boot thing. At the time, it was just flatbread with toppings, cooked on a flat rock, and sliced up for easy eating. It was more of a food for the workin' man, like a plate you could eat.

Still, even though we had the word, we didn't have no sauce. But in 1522, the tomato arrived in Italy. "Thank fuckin' God!" all the Italians said. "We're dyin' for some sauce over here! Plus, the caprese salad is nothin' but cheese." It was the Neapolitans that first started using the tomato. People thought they were poisonous at first, but the Neapolitans said, "Screw it, eat it anyway."

The Taverna del Cerriglio was one of the best places to get the early Neapolitan dish. The soldiers of the Spanish Viceroy came to eat what was then the house special. Can you imagine? Pizza was weird, new, and exotic. (Legend has it that Michelangelo got mugged right outside the Taverna. He was probably in a partial food coma from eating too many slices.)

Over the next couple hundred years or so, pizza spread all over Italy. It was easy and cheap to make. It was considered a peasant dish and was made by the *pizzaioli* (man who makes pizza). By the late 1800s, the King of Italy himself, Umberto I, not only enjoyed pizza in his palace, but had a royal pizzaioli to cook up a few slices whenever he wanted. This must've been very convenient whenever his guys came over to play cards.

The royal family enjoyed three kinds of pizza: one with pork fat, cheese, and basil; one with garlic, oil, and tomatoes; and another with mozzarella, basil, and tomatoes. This last kind of pizza was the favorite of Umberto's queen, Queen Margherita di Savoia. The royal chef, Raffaele Esposito, who had made the pizza with the colors of the Italian flag, named it after the queen. That's where we get Margherita pizzas from—and you just thought it was something on a menu.

It wasn't long afterward that pizza came to America. Most Italians know that the first pizzeria in the

United States was in New York City. It was called
Lombardi's and started selling pizza in 1905. However, Lombardi's actually opened in 1897 as a grocery
store, then started selling pizzas. It also closed for
10 years between 1984 and 1994. There is a pizzeria
in Trenton, New Jersey, called Papa's Tomato Pies
that opened in 1912 and has been open continuously
since, if you want to get technical. And in Chicago,
the Bruno brothers opened a pizza place in 1904, if
you can consider deep-dish real pizza.

But pizza was still an almost exclusively Italian thing
until World War II. Allied troops in Italy discovered
pizza was better than eating MREs. When the war
ended and the troops came home, that's when the big
pizza chains started to open: Pizzeria Uno (opened
1943), Shakey's Pizza (opened 1954), and Pizza Hut
(opened 1958). The next thing you know, everyone's
eating like an Italian. Who could blame them, right?

Why You Gotta Have Good Bread

Imagine Italians without bread. It's almost unthinkable. Yet the Romans didn't even have the right wheat to make flour until sometime in the 5th century BC. The bread was first made by the Greeks, probably around 170 BC. This is probably why the Romans always valued the Greeks; they were always figuring stuff out!

In Roman times, bread would be cooked in a large communal oven. People would have to mark the top of their breads, so when it cooked, they could identify the loaf as theirs. Some of these markings on the top then became associated with a particular kind of bread because of the region or taste or whatever.

Like pasta, Italians have hundreds of bread types. In America, you'll typically see the basic Italian loaf, along with breadsticks, ciabatta, and focaccia. You might even see *muffuletta*, which is a Sicilian bread that makes a great sandwich. It's real big in New Orleans, where a lot of Italian immigrants came into the States.

Some of the breads you may not have heard of are breads like *sgabeo*. It's fried strips of dough that are salted, eaten plain, or stuffed with cheese and ham. Around Christmas, you might see Italians serve *panettone*, which is a sweet bread with raisins and candied fruits. *Coppia ferrarese* looks like twisty bread shaped like an "X" from Ferrara, Italy. You got *borlengo*, or "food of the poor," which is flat and pretty basic stuff, but hey, it's Italian. It's gotta be better than any of that sliced bread you get in the supermarket, right? Then around Easter, you'll see the twisty Easter Bread made with hardboiled eggs baked right in. You pop one out, crack it open, and hey, two foods in one!

So as you can see, for Italians, bread was tied into our earliest origins and our favorite holidays. Plus, everything's got red sauce, so we need something to clean our plate off for salad. Good Italian restaurants always serve good Italian bread. Sure, some places have butter, but the real good places serve their bread with olive oil or maybe some roasted peppers, or why not both? But if an Italian restaurant don't have good bread, it might as well close up shop on the first day. Even the Medigans at the Olive Garden know that!

Don't Forget the Vino!

Even before there was an Italy, the Greeks were making wine in Southern Italy. Back then, they called it Oenotria, meaning "The Land of Wine." Now that's a land I want to visit!

The Romans drank wine every day, and they started to refine the process over the years. They came to understand that aging certain wine made it taste better. The Romans used wooden barrels and glass bottles with corks to hold the wine. Before that, people probably just left their wine in a bucket on the floor!

During the Middle Ages, wine continued to be produced, but sporadically. Weather conditions, wars, and plagues sometimes made wine pretty scarce. By the Renaissance, vineyards were being exported all over the world. Italy was known for making a decent table wine, but people kinda took Italian wine for granted. The quality suffered despite the fact that Italy was exporting lots of wine all over the world.

Soon, there was so much fighting on mainland Italy, who had time for stompin' grapes, am I right? But after the Italian government unified, it stepped in and created classifications for wine. There were standards and regulations wine makers had to adhere to.

There's classifications like *riserva*, which is a wine aged for a minimum amount of time. *Superiore* wine has more alcohol and is of higher quality. There's tons of classifications based on region, the kind of grape, and the kind of wine. You could write a book just on Italian wine. Hell, just the list of the names would fill up a book!

Caesar Salad

The Caesar Salad was not named after Julius Caesar, as most people assume. It was actually invented by an Italian chef named Caesar Cardini in the 1920s. He and his brothers came to America. When Prohibition hit, Caesar opened a place across the border in Tijuana, Mexico, so he could serve booze. They say one night, Caesar's place was packed, and because he was famous for improvising recipes, the recipe was born. Caesar salad became popular amongst the celebrities in Hollywood when he moved his businesses back to the States after Prohibition. Here is Caesar's original recipe for Caesar Salad:

Step 1: Take some crushed garlic and rub it around a wooden salad bowl.

Step 2: Mix ½ teaspoon of salt, 4½ tablespoons of shredded Parmesan cheese, a dash of Worcestershire sauce, 4 tablespoons of olive oil, and 2 eggs that have been boiled for one minute.

Step 3: Toss romaine lettuce in the dressing, preferably the inner leaves.

Step 4: Squeeze a half of a lemon over the whole salad before serving.

Step 5: Garnish with croutons, ground black pepper, and Parmesan cheese.

Sounds good, right? But where's the anchovies? Most people smash up some anchovies with the garlic. Legend has it, Cardini didn't use no anchovies! He thought the fish flavor came out in the Worcestershire. Cardini passed in 1956, so go ahead and use 'em. He won't know.

Ghirardelli Chocolate

Domingo Ghirardelli came to California during the Gold Rush. He tried to find some gold, but found out he was better at making candy. He had several businesses, but candy always seemed to do well for him.

He moved his chocolate factory to a place now called Ghirardelli Square, which is currently a historical landmark. Ghirardelli and his workers discovered the Broma process, which is when you hang a bag of cacao beans in a warm room and let the cocoa butter drip off. Then you use the butter to make your chocolate. This process is how most people make it today.

Over the years, the Ghirardelli Chocolate Factory has been sold to many companies, but it always kept his name. It's like Willy Wonka, only in this case, Willy has been dead since 1894. It's currently owned by a group of Swiss guys, but hey, those guys know chocolate too, right? Thankfully, they had an Italian that could show them the way.

Espresso

If you're up 'til 2 a.m. reading this book and can't sleep, you're probably a big fan of the espresso machine. Naturally, this was built by an Italian. His name was

Angelo Moriondo. Angelo brought his invention to the General Expo of Turin and won bronze. (What won first place, Red Bull?) He got the patent for the first steam-powered espresso machine in 1884, and the machine's been making people jittery ever since.

The only problem with Moriondo's machine is that it made too much coffee. Luigi Bezzerra and Desiderio Pavoni of Milan later patented a machine that made one cup at a time and improved upon the original design. Their 1903 design is much like the espresso machines of today, so remember to thank the Italians next time you hit Starbucks, hipsters.

Nutella

Speaking of hipster favorites, Nutella was another Italian classic. Pietro Ferrero had a bakery in the Piedmont region of Alba, Italy. During World War II, rationing made chocolate scarce, but the Alba area had tons of hazelnuts, so Pietro made a kind of peanut butter, using hazelnuts instead of peanuts.

He used this to extend his chocolate supply. Smart move.

The clever baker sold it as block candy called Pasta Gianduja. Then in 1951, he made a creamy version called Supercrema. Ferrero's son Michele rebranded it as Nutella so it would sell better in Europe. This stuff's so popular, February 5 has been declared World Nutella Day.

The Ferreros' candy company makes all kinds of stuff other than Nutella, including Kinder Chocolates and Tic Tacs. Yeah, they invented Tic Tacs in 1969 so your breath don't stink. Originally called Refreshing Mints, the name was changed based on the sound they make in the box.

The Origin of the Cannoli

Cannoli are so old, they may go back to 1000 AD when the Moors occupied Sicily. It's means "little tube." The singular form is *cannolo*. So you should say

"Leave the gun, take the cannoli," or "Leave the gun and hand me a cannolo."

The dessert was part of the carnival that took place before Lent. Since everyone was going to be suffering for Lent, people wanted to stuff their face with ricotta cheese ahead of time. Cannoli were a symbol of fertility and part of the carnival, which was like the medieval Mardi Gras. So technically, it's a pastry dick. That's probably why the filling's white!

Did Sicilians Invent Donuts?

Almost every culture has fried dough. Who could blame them—it's good, right? Italians have *zeppole*, sometimes called zapes in South Jersey. You can have standard zeppole, which is deep fried dough with a sugar coating, or you could have the ones with anchovies in the middle.

Yeah, I'm not kiddin'. Anchovies. They're an acquired taste, I'll admit.

But if you like donuts, the zeppole can have all kinds of fillings: creams, fruit, chocolate, whatever. Zeppole di San Giuseppe were made for the festival of Saint Joseph in Enna, Sicily, which happens on March 19th. The festival started in Rome around 1479, and this is probably about the same time zeppole popped up.

Tiramisu: That Dessert You Like

It's a classic dessert, right? I mean, you either like your coffee and your cake together or you don't. The invention doesn't go that far back, though. In the 1960s, a restaurant called Le Beccherie in Treviso, Italy, started serving it. Ada Campeol, the then-owner's wife, wanted to make a dessert that would give her energy after the birth of her son. That's why tiramisu means "pick me up" in Italian.

How Italian Is
Pasta Primavera?

Pasta primavera doesn't look like an Italian dish. I mean, it's got pasta, but all those vegetables and pine nuts? The dish was invented in 1975 by Sirio Maccioni in a contest with another chef, although rumor has it that his wife Egidiana actually threw it together in Le Cirque, the famous restaurant the couple owned. While it was invented by Italians, the chef contest was held in Canada and Le Cirque is in America, so it's technically an Italian-American-Canadian dish.

How to Make Sauce

The first thing you do is find an Italian and let them make it. If there's no Italian available or all the Italians are incapacitated, then follow these instructions. The measurements are approximate, but you'll figure it out as you go.

Basic Red Sauce

1 fresh garlic clove	*1 can tomato puree*
1 white onion	*bay leaf*
olive oil, as needed	*fresh basil*
1 can tomato paste	*salt and pepper, to taste*

Step 1: Take a decent-sized pot and put it on the stove.

Step 2: Chop up the garlic and dice the onions.

Step 3: Cover the bottom of the pot with a coating of olive oil and turn on the heat to high.

Step 4: Throw in the onions. Stir them around with a wooden spoon until they're clear.

Step 5: Throw in your garlic, then lower the heat to medium. Stir.

Step 6: Open your cans of tomato paste and puree and pour them in.

Step 7: Chop up the basil and throw that in. Add salt and pepper to taste. Toss in the bay leaf.

Step 8: Once it starts to simmer, turn the heat to the lowest possible setting. Leave the wooden spoon in so it touches the bottom of the pot, stirring occasionally. Let the sauce simmer for two to four hours. If it starts to get a little thick, just throw in a cup of water and stir it in.

It's also advisable to have a good bottle of red wine while you're cooking. Also, have some bread handy; you'll want to dip. Every good chef should test his product, right?

This is your basic red sauce, and it's your ingredients that will make the difference. So make sure you get Italian tomato paste and puree. You want "Antonio's Tomato Paste," not "Bill's Tomato Paste." And don't eat sauce from a jar. God forbid, it's full of sugar! You wanna eat that? You want the natural sweetness of the tomatoes to come out. Speaking of which, here's a few variants on the sauce.

Chunky Tomato Sauce: Instead of tomato puree, use a can of crushed tomatoes. That way you get the nice little chunks. You could also just add fresh tomatoes that you diced or chopped up in a food processor. Nothin' beats Jersey tomatoes. If you're gonna do that, you might want to cook the sauce a little longer than if you use the puree.

Meat Sauce: Duh, add meat! The meat ain't gonna cook in there, so you're gonna have to cook it first. Any pork-related meats will add tons of flavor. A nice greasy pork chop, or some sausage and meatballs.

Mushroom Sauce: If you're one of these people that don't eat meat, I'll pray for you. In the meantime, just add sliced mushrooms to the mix and you got yourself some sauce. Cook the mushrooms at least part of the way first in some olive oil and garlic, then dump the whole pan in the pot. More olive oil ain't gonna hurt it.

Pizza Sauce: Instead of basil, use oregano.

Spicy Sauce: Add red pepper flakes, and lots of 'em. If you can get your hands on some long hots, dice 'em up real good, cook 'em in a little olive oil, and dump the whole pan in the sauce.

How to Make Meatballs

It's real simple. You may not even need an Italian to attempt this yourself. All the measurements are approximate so just wing it or consult with the nearest Italian grandma.

Ingredients:

Ground beef, veal, and pork (the meatloaf pack at your local supermarket is perfect)

white onion

parsley

Italian bread crumbs

Parmesan cheese

garlic powder

one egg

salt

olive oil

Step 1: Dice the onion and parsley really fine.

Step 2: Put all the ingredients in a bowl except the olive oil. You want about ¾ cup of bread crumbs and a good healthy sprinkle of Parmesan and garlic powder. If it's too dry, add another egg. If it's too mushy, add more bread crumbs. It ain't rocket science.

Step 3: Mix the ingredients with your hands, because that's how real Italians cook.

Step 4: Make meatballs about the size you want. Slightly bigger than a golf ball is about right. You can make them the size of baseballs if you want, but then they take forever to cook. And you got a life to lead, right?

Step 5: Put some olive oil in a pan and lightly fry the meatballs. It's gonna be a greasy mess, so be prepared. Have some paper towels on a plate to dab off your balls.

Step 6: Drop the meatballs in your sauce. If you made extra, freeze them for later. If you have leftover sauce, you can also freeze that for later.

Italian Pro Tip: If you got some leftover bread from a couple of days before, chop it up in your food processor and make your own bread crumbs.

🦋🦋🦋

How to Boil Pasta

Follow the directions on the box, genius. If you needed to read this part, you're really in trouble!

Italian Pro Tip: Drop half a teaspoon of olive oil in the water, and your pasta won't stick.

CHAPTER THREE

America Wasn't Cool Until the Italians Came

Let's face it, things can get pretty boring without some Italians to liven things up. America started out as basically another version of England. The Founding Fathers knew they were gonna need some guys with balls if they were gonna form a new country.

Colonial Times

You all know who Thomas Jefferson is, but you may not have heard of his good buddy, Philip Mazzei. Like

Jefferson, Mazzei was a brainiac. He was a doctor, farmer, and businessman who met Jefferson and Ben Franklin in Europe. Jefferson convinced him to come to America and start the first commercial vineyard, which he did. No surprise one of the first Italians in America got to work making red wine as soon as possible.

Mazzei was all over the Revolutionary War. In fact, the phrase "all men are created equal" may have actually been Mazzei's idea. He and Jefferson frequently brainstormed ideas in letters, and Mazzei had written the phrase in a letter in Italian some time prior to the publication of the Declaration of Independence.

See that? Italians practically invented America!

The good doctor helped out in the war effort by being a secret agent. He was sent abroad to borrow money from the Grand Duke of Tuscany and he purchased and shipped arms to the American rebels to help the war. But after the war, Mazzei couldn't stay in the States. There were no Italian restaurants and no good places to get bread yet.

Frances Vigo was another Italian-American patriot. He was a secret agent for General George Rogers Clark. Unfortunately, he got caught by American Indians that had allied with the British. Technically, he was a Spanish citizen, so the Brits let him go under the condition that he promised "not to do anything injurious to the British interests on his way to St. Louis." He was an honorable guy, so he didn't, but once he reached St. Louis he turned around and hightailed it back to Clark to blab.

Vigo also had a little bit of money. Since America was new, the Continental Dollar wasn't exactly welcomed. Vigo, however, helped out Clark by exchanging the notes for gold and silver coins. Big mistake. The government stiffed him, but ended up paying back his estate after he was dead.

On the upside, Vigo stuck around after the war and eventually established Jefferson Academy in Vincennes, Indiana. Today it's called Vincennes University. In 1818, Indiana established Vigo County, which is named after this patriot. They should've renamed Indiana as Vigo. Then we could have the

Vigo 500, Vigo-opolis, and the Vigo Pacers. Way better names.

Italian Unification

When Italy was finally unified into one country, the Italian constitution and the structure of the government heavily favored Northern Italy. The Southern Italians, already poorer and essentially just coming out of a system that was mostly feudal, were hit hard. The poverty in the 1880s drove millions out of Italy. Approximately 4.5 million Italian immigrants would come to America between 1876 and 1924. (No wonder they needed a whole island in New York harbor to process everyone.) And Little Italy didn't just appear in New York—the towns popped up in many of the major cities in the United States and in countries as diverse as Ireland, China, Chile, and Kenya. What can I say? We Italians get around.

The Civil War

One of the earliest Italian communities was Little Palermo in New Orleans, appearing right before the Civil War. This community was made up of Sicilians who sometimes smuggled goods past the various blockades in and out of the city during the war.

In 1890, a New Orleans police chief met with a mysterious accident and Italians, being the new immigrants, got blamed. There was a trial, but things got out of hand and an angry mob broke into the prison and lynched 11 Italians. Where do they get off? This was right around the time the word "Mafia" first appeared in print in the United States.

✖✖✖

Ellis Island: Where Everybody Got a Nickname

There was a big spike in Italians coming to the States, starting around 1876 and ending around 1930. From 1892 to 1954, immigrants came in to New York through Ellis Island. Lots of people think Italians got the nickname "wop" because at Ellis Island, you could be called out for entering "without passport" or "without papers," abbreviated "w.o.p." It actually may come from the word *guappo*, which in Neapolitan means "pimp" or "thug" or "braggart." Either way, if you like your teeth, don't call an Italian a wop.

Something like five million *paisans* hopped a boat looking for work in America. Lots of people think they were also looking for a new life in America, but that ain't necessarily true. Something like 50 percent of the Italian immigrants that came here between 1901 and 1920 said "fuck it," and went home after making some money. They didn't want to learn English and they didn't want to assimilate. When they went back, a lot of them had the money to buy land so they could have their own farms. They also probably missed the good olive oil and cannoli.

....

paisan/paesan. same as goomba, meaning fellow countryman, comrade.

Hey, paisan! Come by, we're playin' cards!
....

Most of the people that came were called *contadini*, which means "farmer" or "laborer." This is a time when most people grew their own food, so that makes sense. Only about 20 percent of the immigrants were skilled craftsmen right off the boat. And something like 80 percent of the immigrants came from the more Southern regions of Italy, like Sicily and Calabria. The peak happened in 1913, when some of the Northern Italians started to get in on the action. By 1920, Italians were the largest immigrant population working in mines in the United States. They were just like the Mexicans are now, coming here and working their asses off.

But you couldn't just show up—the Italians had a network. In the US, there would be what Italians called a *padrone*, which means "master." He was an Italian that already lived in America, knew the lay of the land, and could tell you what stores sold good pasta and bread. A guy like that was key in helping new immigrants make their way. Y'see, it always helps to know a guy!

World War II

For obvious reasons, immigrants didn't make it out of Italy too often during and right before the war. Il Douchebag saw to that. Italian-Americans didn't have it nearly as bad as the German-Americans or Japanese-Americans during the war, but people get bent out of shape about all kinds of things. On the West Coast, Italian fisherman had their boats confiscated because the American government thought some Italians would pass messages in the boats as spies. Even Giuseppe DiMaggio, father of the great baseball player Joe DiMaggio, got his boat confiscated. How are you supposed to catch the seven fishes with no boat, huh? It's bullshit.

There were other stupid rules. Some Italians even got put into internment camps like the Japanese did, although not nearly as many. Restrictions against Italian nationals in the US were lifted on Columbus Day, 1942. When Italy surrendered to the Allies, almost all the internees were released after September 8, 1943. About friggin' time. Can you imagine being locked up just because you were Italian?

. . . .

vaffanculo. fuck off, or fuck you.

"You don't like the Godfather *movies? Vaffanculo!"*

. . . .

Americans insisted that Italians all speak English, which you may or may not agree with. *Vaffanculo!* How are we supposed to curse, huh? *Butana!* Isn't it better to curse in another language the Medigan kids don't know?

. . . .

butana. exclamation of surprise; the exact translation is "whore."

"Butana! This line in the DMV hasn't moved in an hour!"

. . . .

But after the war, Italians were glad the Americans came in and liberated them. Not that we weren't going to get around to it. Still, lots of Italian-Americans fought in the war, so by the end of it all, we kinda came out pretty even.

Immigration After World War II

The post-war years were a good time to get your ass to the States. For the next 25 years, Italy was one of the main avenues for immigrants coming to the United States. Plus, there were so many Italians already here for several generations. We're big on family, so we like to have lots of kids.

In the 1950s, the greasers were all the rage. Everyone wanted to dress like the Fonz with leather jackets, motorcycles, and hair in a pompadour. This trend came out of the working class neighborhoods, which were made up of a lot of Italians. It was all about the hair, and since Italians got the best hair, we were naturally the best greasers. And while the kids were listening to cool stuff like Bobby Darin and the Four Seasons, the adults were listening to the Rat Pack and Tony Bennett. You couldn't turn on a radio without hearing an Italian voice come out of it!

In 1965, LBJ changed the rules and even more immigrants could come to America. By 1970, things in Italy started to bounce back, so with money in the Old Country, Italian immigration declined. But hey, by that time, the US had Al Pacino, track suits, and Chef Boyardee. (Not that I would eat pasta from a can, but the Medigans in the Midwest don't know the difference. Plus, Hector Boyardee was an Italian immigrant, so he meant well.)

By the 1980s, there were way more immigrants coming from Mexico and Asia than from Europe. Italians continued to make America cool. Madonna practically ran the music industry back then and you don't get more Italian than her. Okay, she was a little bit of a *schifozz*, but you gotta do that stuff to sell records now.

....

schifozz. short for *schifoso* or *schifoas*; disgusting, gross, filthy.

> *That guy that stole your purse was a drug addict that abandoned his kids. What a schifozz.*

....

During the 1990s, Italy relaxed its immigration laws, so not only did fewer Italians come to the US, but more people from other countries went to Italy. Who could blame them? You ever see the suits and shoes you can buy there?

It was clear that Italian-Americans were a vital part of the USA. In the late '90s, 82 of 1,000 of the largest American cities had Italian mayors. Italian-Americans went to space and some of them were ladies, too! Jay Leno, an Italian, hosted the *Tonight Show*. Antonin Scalia and Samuel Alito were on the Supreme Court. Amazing, right? And I know what you're saying...

So, how do we not have an Italian president yet? I know! It's an outrage! Rudolph Giuliani ran, but that stunad wasn't gonna win. Geraldine Ferraro, the first woman to run on a presidential ticket, was Italian.

But she ran with Walter Mondale, whose ancestors put the "white" in "white bread," so that wasn't gonna happen. Who do we got to run at this point? Can you say "President Stallone"? Think about it! A Stallone/De Niro ticket would lock up the Italian-American vote! And if De Niro's got too many movies to make, you got Nicholas Cage or Leonardo DiCaprio as backups. Think about it, Sly!

CHAPTER FOUR

Family: The Only People That Put Up with Your Shit

Bigger Is Better

Most Italian-Americans are Catholic, so for many years, if you were gonna give your wife the badda-bing, no contraception was required. That created a lot of Italians, so big families just tended to happen. And if your immediate family was big, then it was likely your parents' immediate family was big, so you have a ton of cousins, too. In the old days, havin' that many kids meant plenty of help on the farm. These days, it just means you gotta be smart and get a scholarship if you wanna go to college.

Boss of the Family: Men vs. Women

In the old days, the oldest male was the boss, and in a traditional Italian family, that still holds true today. But Italians also got some strong-willed women, make no mistake. You know who I mean—that aunt of yours that bosses everyone around at Christmas, or maybe it's your mother, who's not afraid to slap you across the head when you take the Lord's name in vain.

But most importantly, in an Italian family, there is great respect for the elders. Grandparents take care of the little ones, and you don't leave your grandparents in some home run by the State. Unless you hate 'em for some reason, and even then, it's just wrong. Even the adults will consult with the elders for important decisions. There's a lot of wisdom in age, and Italians recognize that fact.

So listen to your nana. Eat something!

Sunday Dinner

Italian Sunday dinner is an important weekly event, and it happens early, usually around 2 or 3 p.m. Typically it's Italian food, some kind of pasta and meat. Red sauce, meatballs, and sausage are your standards, served along with a good *braciole*. To mix it up, your ma might go with a white sauce once in a while: clams, and maybe shrimp. If your nana is really looking to impress, she might make chicken or veal Parmesan along with the pasta. Pretty much anything you've ever seen on an Italian restaurant's menu is a possibility, so if you're ever invited to dinner, do not eat a snack ahead of time!

Sunday dinner is family time. It's a time where everyone bonds and shares things. Yeah, it might seem that everyone is yelling and talking over each other, but that's just our way. To miss a family dinner is an insult, so you'd better have a good excuse. Quite frankly, you'd have to be nuts to miss food this good. It's usually the best meal of the week!

....

braciole. an Italian dish consisting of flank steak rolled up with spices, cheeses, and hard-boiled egg, which is then served in spaghetti sauce.

This braciole is good, but you forgot to take the tooth-picks out!

....

Living at Home

In the old days, large extended Italian families would live together. Why not? Saves you the trip on Sunday. Plus, when you're tight with your family, they don't mind adult children hanging around. Sure, some might call you a "mama's boy" for living at home as an adult, but it can take years to find an Italian wife to cook sauce like your ma, and it can take even longer to properly train a Medigan.

That isn't to say you're gonna sit on your ass all day. Italians value a work ethic. This goes back to their days on the farm. You might be living with the folks, but you better pull your own weight, whether it's working a 9 to 5 job, helping out in the family business, or writing a hilarious coffee table book about being an Italian while living in your parents' basement.

Weddings

There's nothing better than an Italian wedding. It combines everything an Italian family is about: religion, family, and food. Italian families will use almost anything as an excuse to throw a party, and a wedding reception is a good one. Everyone gets dressed up, you get to see all your cousins, and you get church out of the way for the week! Italian weddings are truly a family event, as most of the bridesmaids and groomsmen end up being your relatives.

If you're looking for a family that will spend way too much money on a wedding, an Italian family will go all out. Italians got a high bar for food, so forget the meat and fish option bullshit. There's going to be *antipasto* like you won't believe, then Italian entrees that will probably include some pasta, and since every Italian knows a good baker or two, don't miss cake. Since more than half your relatives make their own wine, there will be plenty of bottles of that at every table. And while an open bar will always be a highlight at any reception, the espresso bar at the end will blow your local Starbucks away.

....

antipasto. Italian appetizer plate that usually has meat, cheeses, olives, anchovies, and other Italian delicacies.

   Get the antipasto ready before Mario gets here, I want to have some before that fat fuck eats it all.
....

The bride will come around for cards, usually stuffed with money, or there'll be a birdcage where people can drop off their envelope. Two of the larger cousins will guard that birdcage with their lives. Jordan almonds are a traditional wedding favor. Five almonds for the bride and groom symbolize health, wealth, happiness, fertility, and longevity for the happy couple. Plus, who don't like free candy?

gabbadost. stubborn, hardheaded.

My mother refuses to learn email. She's a little gabbadost.

The Tarantella is also going to play. It's the Italian song where everyone gets up and dances in a circle. The song originated in Southern Italy and has been played at Italian weddings since there's been Italians. When the song plays, don't be *gabbadost*. Get up and dance!

Funerals

When you're from a big Italian family, on any given month, if there isn't a wedding or someone's communion party, you're probably going to a funeral. These days, an Italian funeral probably won't differ much from any standard Catholic funeral you've ever attended.

In the old days, a body might be laid out in the home for a few days. People would come to the deceased's house, comfort the family, and eat a lot of food. (Everyone would bring food.) Then there'd be a ceremony at the church, a ride to the cemetery, one last bit at the gravesite and then—boom—in the hole.

As the family would leave the gravesite, they might drop a handful of dirt or a flower on the deceased. This is a tradition that's still practiced today. In the Old Country, you might have worried about the dead guy's soul not leaving to go to Heaven. The symbolism behind the flower arrangements these days pays homage to that. You might have an arrangement with a picture of the Gates of Heaven or a crescent moon. This is to tell the soul, "Hey, stupid! You're dead! Fly up to heaven!"

Modern Italian-Americans will do the viewing at a funeral parlor, then a church service the next day, a ride past the dead guy's house and/or place of business, then to the cemetery for the final goodbye. Afterward, the family will invite you to a nice restaurant, probably on par with something used for a wedding. The dinner won't be as elaborate, but the food will be top notch. Then everyone will have a drink and talk about old times. Who wants to be depressed all day, right?

Everyone's Family in an Italian Family

Italians like people and the more, the merrier. When you become friends with an Italian, chances are, you'll be treated like family. It's just the way we are. If you "know a guy" that does you a favor, you return the favor by having him eat with the family! Besides, what's one more folding chair at the dinner table, right? There's plenty of pasta for all. If you seem like an okay person and your Italian friend vouches for you, you join the club.

That isn't to say that Italians don't have their share of stunads and scumbags in the family tree. But with all the talking we do, it's hard to keep a secret from the rest of the family. Eventually, one of your relatives is going to straighten you out, or at least let everyone around you loudly know how stupid you are. It's also hard to stay a scumbag when everyone in the family knows your business.

I'm not sayin' Italians are perfect (but we're pretty close). The thing is, good relationships have to have good communication. And since no one ever shuts up in an Italian household, the communication never stops!

CHAPTER FIVE

There Is No Mafia (But If There Were, Here's What We'd Know)

Pinpointing the exact time and place where this terrible rumor started is nearly impossible. With all the great things Italians got going for them, it was natural that a few people would be jealous, right? It's all just bullshit gossip that got turned into some very good movies and TV shows. Just keep in mind, this entire chapter don't mean nothin'.

The Sicilian Vespers

No, not Vespas, stunad, *Vespers*! Back in 1282, Sicily was just a big island that other kingdoms kept invading. During that time, the Angevin French occupied it. The Sicilians kind of grudgingly tolerated the French presence until Easter Day in Palermo. On that day, a French soldier insulted a Sicilian woman on the street. Needless to say, the Sicilian men would not let that stand. It probably went down something like this:

"What did that French asshole say?!"

"Tomaso, it was nothing! Don't make trouble, you'll get hurt!"

"Don't tell me what to do, Marie! It don't concern you! It's about honor! Now what did that French douchebag do, Vito?!"

"I'm pretty sure he insulted her, Tomaso. You know, I'm gettin' sick of these French assholes. What the fuck is a crepe anyway? It's like a taco fucked a dessert and had a baby!"

"I'm with you. Let's get the crew together and teach Frenchie and those beret-wearing motherfuckers a lesson they won't forget, huh?!"

"Please, Tomaso, don't! This is a holy day!"

"Go home, Marie!"

Anyhow, the resistance fighters to the French were called the Sicilian Vespers, and on that Easter, the shit hit the fan. Over six weeks, the Vespers killed 3,000 French people, and Charles I, the installed French-born king, lost control of the island. Fuck you, Chuck! Not so mouthy now, are ya?

Vespers, by the way, is what they called the evening prayer before Easter. You're supposed to give thanks for the day and make an evening sacrifice of praise to God. Well, the Sicilians decided to sacrifice some French guys instead.

Anyhow, the Sicilians asked the Pope to let them run things themselves, but at that time, the Pope was French. Fortunately, some Sicilians knew a guy: Peter III of Aragon. Peter was a king without a kingdom, just a big armada of ships. He sailed to Sicily, and bada boom, bada bing, he became the new king.

The Sicilian Vespers may or may not have disbanded, depending on how you look at it. These were men of high honor, and they taught that to their sons. So in a sense, the Vespers never left Sicily. They would always be there to rise up and adapt to the situation.

La Garduña, Camorra, and Gabelloti

Around 1417, there was a medieval prison gang from Spain that called itself *La Garduña*. They grew into an organized crime syndicate of robbers, arsonists, kidnappers, and assassins. These guys were so badass and ruthless, they actually worked for the Inquisition.

Needless to say, you wouldn't want to mess with their tapas, if you know what I mean.

The Treaty of Blois put Naples in control of Spain, and La Garduña saw opportunity. Whether they introduced their secret organization to the Neapolitans or whether the Neapolitan *Camorra* already existed, no one knows for sure. But both groups were very secret societies with blood oaths and ceremonies and hooded cloaks and shit.

At the same time, Spanish noblemen owned Italy, but they didn't actually live there. So the Spaniards hired land managers called *Gabelloti*, and as long as the noblemen weren't around, the Gabelloti were in charge. This was a big deal at a time when people lived in feudal societies and had to grow their own food. The Spanish occupiers also didn't care about the locals, so the Gabelloti were the only guys around that might deliver them some justice if things went wrong. Of course, a little justice might cost ya, or you might owe someone a favor. Sound familiar?

So, you combine the Vespers, the men of honor who hated all occupiers of Sicily, with the criminal gangs and the land managers who pulled the local strings. Now you got a network. An organization, if you will.

Lots of organized crime families had similar roots within their own ethnic groups. The Chinese Triads started out as a resistance group that wanted to restore the Ming Dynasty. The Yakuza were a combination of Ronin samurai, professional gamblers, and merchants who had to find a new way to make a living during the Edo Period. The Red Mafya traces its origins back to Russian prison gangs and ex-soldiers looking to make a buck.

But as Italians, we just can't help being the best at what we do, even when what we do is bad. So if the Mafia existed (which it don't), it set the stage for how to run an organized crime family in the world.

The Black Hand

In the early and mid-1800s, Italy went through a lot of turmoil. Guys like Giuseppe Mazzini were trying to unite the whole boot through a secret organization called the Carbonari. Overthrowing your own king ain't no small thing, so it was probably natural that Mazzini worked with other secret Italian organizations at the time.

The word Mafia wasn't even a common term yet. It first appeared in 1863 in an opera called *The Mafiosi of the Vicaria*, but the word was only in the title. It's never even mentioned in the show! (That's how much the Mafia was secret, but then again, it's pretty easy to be a secret when you don't exist.)

The Black Hand first appeared in the States in 1869, in New Orleans. These Sicilian gentlemen blackmailed the local Italian populace. One of their guys would deliver you a letter with a black handprint or a dagger or a little cartoon of a bomb on it. The Italians knew what that symbol meant. It meant that if you didn't pay up, an "accident" would happen to you or your storefront. For instance, a lit stick of dynamite might get mysteriously thrown through your window. Hey, it's a dangerous world.

Of course, if you paid, there was no problem, so most people paid.

New York was another place where the Black Hand operated. In 1881, Giuseppe Esposito was one of the first made guys to enter the US. He and his crew had murdered some landowners back in Sicily, so they came to New York, fled to New Orleans, but eventually got extradited back to Italy.

....

made guy. an official, inducted member of the Mafia that swears an oath of loyalty to their crime family above all else.

Joey became a made guy, so now we can make some real money!
....

And remember back on page 61 when I told you about the Italians getting lynched in New Orleans in 1890? Well, I failed to mention that if the Mafia did exist, that police chief that got whacked may have gotten killed in the crossfire between two rival Mafia families. That's still no excuse to lynch people.

The Clutch Hand

The first big Mafia crime family in the USA was started by Giuseppe "the Clutch Hand" Morello in the 1890s. He was called that because he had a deformed hand. Morello ran the 107th Street Mob in New York, which would eventually become the Morello Crime Family. (Joseph Valachi, the first made guy to flip to the Feds, actually whacked Morello in 1930.) The Morello Family went through a few name changes over the years and is now known as the Genovese Crime Family of New York.

Prohibition and the Mustache Petes

In Italy, Italians knew there was a difference between Camorra, the Black Hand, and the Mafia, but the Medigans just lumped them all into "the Mafia" in America. By the early 1900s, the members of the Black Hand or old school Mafia were called the Mustache Petes. These guys were richer than other Italian immigrants they extorted, but they weren't *rich* rich, ya know?

When Prohibition hit, there was a lot of money in bootleg booze. (Sorta like the way illegal drugs are very lucrative today.) The more ruthless mobsters quickly gravitated toward these easy gains, but the Mustache Petes didn't like it. Bootlegging brought in more profit, but way more heat from the cops. The split between traditional Sicilian Mafia and Sicilian-America Mafia became a huge rift.

You see, old school Sicilians didn't care about money first. They were big on secrecy, honor, and vendettas. The Sicilian mobsters never engaged in prostitution. They considered it beneath them and a dishonorable enterprise. The Sicilian-American mobsters, however, were all about the money. Bootlegging? Sure! Prostitution? Why not?

Eventually, the Mustache Petes became an impediment to the up-and-coming Lucky Lucianos of the world. Some retired, but those that didn't met with mysterious and unfortunate accidents. The money just poured in. Al Capone was said to be worth $100 million, and that's in the 20s! His net worth in today's dollars? Try $1.3 *billion*. That's a lot of *escarole!*

....

escarole. a leafy green vegetable that tastes like a bitter lettuce, which is sometimes used in Italian dishes.

If you want to cook escarole and beans like my mother, you need more garlic, Marie!
....

Madonn', the Money!

The Mafia was rolling in it during Prohibition. Early on, the Irish Families put up a fight, but they were outgunned and outnumbered. Mussolini was driving the Mafia out of Italy, and guess where they all went? The Jewish gangs worked with the Mafia, but even most of these guys got pushed out or retired. The Mafia was a Sicilian-only club, and that's the way bootlegging was gonna run.

In May 1929, every major crime figure went to Atlantic City for the Atlantic City Conference to discuss their problems. It was decided that in order to lower the heat on everyone, Al Capone would go to jail on a small weapon's charge. (Capone would run things from his very well-appointed cell in Philadelphia's Eastern State Penitentiary.) But the second biggest thing they discussed was getting out of the bootlegging business. Every major family got out of making booze months before it became legal again.

By this time, Lucky Luciano became the most powerful Mafia boss in history. He created the Commission so that the families could settle their disputes rather than go to war and lose money. This saved them even more money on top of the millions they had already made.

But the Mafia ain't run by investment bankers. It's run by guys who are, shall we say, rather impulsive. Bugsy Siegel got everyone to invest in Las Vegas. The place was a bust at first, and by the time Bugsy started showing a profit, the Commission decided that his dividend would be a bullet to the head.

Lucky was still running the show, but from outside the country. The US government had put him away on a pandering charge. But during World War II, the officials were worried about supplying the troops out of the New York docks. There were some fires and a few of those supplies "fell off the truck." The US government cut a deal with Lucky since the Mafia controlled the docks; if all their problems disappeared, they'd spring him from the joint and deport him back to Italy after the war. Little did they know that it was Lucky causing all the problems in the first place! The balls on that guy!

The 1960s: The Peak

Things peaked for the Mafia in the US right around this time. The money from Prohibition meant that the remaining families were already rich and then made even more money on top of that. They owned legitimate businesses and controlled national unions. They owned politicians, bribed cops, and were making more money than they knew what to do with!

Then in 1957, Boss Vito Genovese got the bright idea to have another meeting of the Commission. This time the meeting was to be held in Apalachin, New York. Things were going so well, Vito! Why?

Ya see, Vito wasn't that old school. More American-ized bosses had risen in the ranks and now controlled things. Much like the Mustache Petes had been pushed out by the Lucky Lucianos, the old guard was now being pushed out by guys like Genovese who had even less respect for the rules. These guys were more reckless and brazen than the previous bosses. The cops stumbled in on the meeting, and 58 made guys ended up arrested. It was a complete embarrassment for the Genoveses, and no family with any sense ever wanted to attend a Commission meeting again.

Then Joe Valachi testified before Congress about the existence of the Mafia, its secret traditions and crimes, and it blew the doors wide open. Despite the $100,000 bounty on his head, he continued to live in prison until he died of a heart attack in 1971. But any pretense of a "secret society" was gone. Every Medigan with a television knew about the Mafia! It did not bode well for the future.

Today's Mafia: Not to be Trifled With

The Mafia is now the most well-known secret criminal organization in the world (if it existed). In less than 100 years, the Mafia went from being something that only Sicilians right off the boat knew about to... well, who ain't seen *The Godfather* and *The Sopranos* at this point, right?

In the 1980s, the Feds came down on John Gotti like a bag of hammers. Ralph Natale, a Philadelphia boss, became the first Mafia boss to flip for the Feds. With everyone racing to cut a deal, it was kind of hard to keep a criminal organization afloat.

Technology made it almost impossible to keep anything a secret. The Families had to resort to more and more extreme schemes to stay out of jail. Vincent Gigante pretended he was mentally ill and managed to stay out of prison for almost 30 years. Labeled the Oddfather by the press, Gigante ran the Genovese

Family but eventually, the Feds got him, too. He cut a plea deal, something else Mafia bosses almost never did, but it was to keep other relatives out of prison.

Today's made guys have gone back to keeping a low profile. Gotti was the last of the flashy bosses. These days Mafia guys make less money than previous generations. No one wants to be boss anymore because the boss is always targeted by the Feds. Families resort to promoting "decoy bosses" or avoiding making anyone an official boss at all. Competition from other immigrant groups, including the Mexican drug cartels and Red Mafya, is fierce and now it's the Mafia that's outnumbered and outgunned.

But make no mistake, you don't mess with these guys. Ever. Just because there's not that many anymore don't mean they ain't dangerous. Some families have invested their money wisely and still control significant turf. No longer does the Mafia control unions and politicians. These days, they control sports gambling and commit credit card fraud. Italian immigrants and their descendants now have legitimate opportunities in America and the RICO makes the Mafia lifestyle too dangerous. The desperation that once drove Italians into organized crime is gone.

Assuming that the Mafia ever existed, which it don't.

CHAPTER SIX

Teaching Medígans

Non-Italians can be thrown when they meet Italians for the first time. Let's face it, we can be pretty intense and loud sometimes. You might wanna prepare your quiet, Christian girlfriend from white-bread Ohio for meeting your family. Here are a couple of tips to smooth the way.

Using Nicknames

We like nicknames. Usually they come out of some shorthand for questioning a situation in a sarcastic manner. Again, the end goal is usually just to cut to the chase. But a lot of times, those nicknames can stick, and it's a colorful thing that you may like or be haunted by the rest your life.

Question: "You know what you're doin' there, Einstein?"

Translation: I think you may be in over your head because I don't think you're smart enough to perform this task, but I'm here to help.

Question: "Where'd you learn to drive, Stevie Wonder? At a school for the blind?"

Translation: You drive like an idiot.

Question: "Hey, Gordon Ramsay, we gonna eat tonight or what?"

Translation: Hurry up with the food, I'm hungry.

Question: "Yo! DJ Jazzy Jeff! You wanna turn down the music? I'm tryin' to watch the game here!"

Translation: Turn down your music, I can't hear the game.

Getting Emotional

Italians can get angry like anyone else. The level of anger is proportionate to how directly or indirectly we may be threatening you.

Anger Level Tomei: "That better not be what I think it is."

Anger Level Liotta: "You got about three seconds to explain yourself."

Anger Level Pacino: "You think I'm angry?! You haven't *seen* angry!"

Anger Level De Niro: "You think I won't hit you? Huh?! Huh?!"

Anger Level Pesci: "You're dead! Ya hear me?! Dead!"

But don't get me wrong, Italian attitude isn't just anger. In many ways, what you see as anger is just us blowing off steam. It's really that we're complaining about you right in front of you when you do something stupid. Hey, at least we're not talking behind your back, right?

And while we're not afraid to say something when things go wrong, we're also not afraid to compliment people when things go right.

Phrase: "Look at this guy! Is he beautiful or what?"
Translation: I am very pleased with this person.

Phrase: "This guy makes the best Italian red. He's the king. The absolute king."
Translation: This guy makes really good red wine. It's unsurpassed.

Phrase: "Madonn'! The cannoli!"
Translation: Wow, these are great cannoli!

Phrase: "Ha! This guy! Huh? This guy!"
Translation: This guy is the best.

Sarcasm Ain't Personal

Italians can be pretty sarcastic. (Yeah, right. Like you didn't know that!) And while that's just how a lot of us talk, we don't usually mean nothin' mean by it. But to the new person in the room whose family didn't laugh in their face and break their balls every time they fucked up, it might come as a shock. Medigans gotta know it's just our way. Nothin' personal.

Italians value respect, and we know it's rude and disrespectful to get in someone's face. Still, we got shit to do, and being straightforward means we don't have a problem talking to someone when we need them. And if they're not listening or paying attention, we don't have a problem shouting, "Oh! Let's get a waiter over here! While I'm young, huh?"

Now, you may be lucky enough to encounter Italians in your daily life. It's important to distinguish what our attitude means. For instance, we might ask you a question, but it don't necessarily mean what you think. Here are some translations of commonly used phrases:

Question: "Oh! What are you? The Pope?"

Translation: Don't be so high and mighty. You're a little full of yourself.

Question: "You're shittin' me, right?"

Translation: I can't believe what you just said. Please clarify or repeat.

Question: "Do you honestly expect me to believe you made this pizza?"

Translation: I don't believe you made this pizza.

Question: "Are you fuckin' kidding me?!"

Translation: I am shocked and appalled. This can't be true!

You might ask, where does this attitude come from? Does it come from Italy? Yeah, sure, that's definitely part of it. Italians right off the boat ain't no wallflowers. But in the US, over 25 percent of Italian-Americans, that's 4.2 million, live in either New York or New

Jersey (according to the 2005–2007 census data). No surprise that's where the good pizza is.

But as you probably already know, New York and New Jersey can be a little intense. So maybe that's why Italians got attitude to spare. You try and keep your patience taking the Verrazano Bridge at rush hour every day and see if you don't start to develop an edge!

Dating: The Guys

If you're dating an Italian guy and you're a Medigan, you might watch out for some key phrases.

Phrase: "What are you? A model or something?"
Translation: You're very pretty.

Phrase: "I don't mean to brag, but I think you're gonna like my car."
Translation: I'm expecting you to say something nice about my car.

Phrase: "I don't take just anyone to this place."

Translation: I take all my dates here.

Phrase: "I'm not lookin' for a relationship right now. Let's just have fun."

Translation: You're not Catholic. I can't marry you, but we can have a ton of sex.

So if you're a Medigan and you want to respond like an Italian, you gotta use reactions that Italians understand.

Phrase: "What are you? A model or something?"

Reply: "Yeah, I'm Kate Fucking Upton. You can just say I'm hot."

Phrase: "I don't mean to brag, but I think you're gonna like my car."

Reply: "Good, I don't wanna ride in a P.O.S."

Phrase: "I don't take just anyone to this place."

Reply: "You're so full of shit."

Phrase: "I'm not lookin' for a relationship right now. Let's just have fun."

Reply: "I can get Netflix and chill any time I want. If you like it, put a ring on it. Don't treat me like some butana you just met."

Italian men like to test the limits. You have to draw the line and challenge them verbally or dating is no fun.

Dating: The Girls

If you're dating an Italian woman and you're a Medigan, she's probably tired of all the goombas she usually dates. You might be a nice change. Still, an Italian woman might come off as a little brash unless you got the inside scoop.

Phrase: "Is this place you're taking me to nice or what?"
Translation: I don't like cheap dates.

Phrase: "Don't take this the wrong way, but I've been inside better cars."
Translation: You're car's not so great, but I won't hold it against you.

Phrase: "I don't play games. I'm not into drama, so be straight with me."

Translation: I am totally into games. I am definitely into drama and I will test you a lot.

Phrase: "You live by yourself, right?"

Translation: If you're married, you'd better tell me. If you gotta girlfriend, you'd better dump her for me.

Medigan guys, you gotta respond with confidence. That's a rule for all women.

Phrase: "Is this place you're taking me to nice or what?"

Reply: "It's the best, you're gonna love it!"

Phrase: "Don't take this the wrong way, but I've been inside better cars."

Reply: "This thing is vintage! They don't make 'em like this anymore!"

Phrase: "I don't play games. I'm not into drama, so be straight with me."

Reply: "Whoa. Relax. I'm an honest guy!"

Phrase: "You live by yourself, right?"

Reply: "Yeah, swear ta God! Let's just have fun."

Ten Things You Should Never Do on a Date with an Italian

1. **Show up with bad hair.** If you don't have decent hair, the date is going nowhere.

2. **Be cheap.** Italians like to flash a little cash on a date. Tip well.

3. **Set foot in an Olive Garden.** If you're a Medigan, stay away from any chain Italian restaurant. Ask any Italian and he'll point you the way to a nice place.

4. **Ask for directions.** Italians are very big on getting to places in a short amount of time. Map out your route ahead of time to impress you date. GPS is for pussies.

5. Be disrespectful to anyone. Italians like to give respect and get it. You know, unless the other person is an asshole.

6. Talk too much. Unless you're also Italian, this will be impossible anyway. Also, don't ask if we're in the Mafia or know someone in the Mafia. There is no Mafia and if there were, we don't tell Medigans anything.

7. Bad-mouth famous Italians. Sinatra, De Niro, Pacino, and even Stallone. If you don't like 'em, just don't go there.

8. Back down from a confrontation. Italians live for confrontation, so whether it's arguing over an insult or a parking space, grow a pair if you're on a date.

9. Be nervous. Most Italians are very confident, so if you're a Medigan, you gotta ask "WWAID (What would an Italian do)?" Be bold.

10. Schedule it for Sunday. Sunday is family dinner day. Unless you've been dating long enough to get an invite, pick a different day. If you do get an invite, be prepared to eat *a lot*. There will be no dieting around older Italian ladies.

Living with an Italian: Dos and Don'ts

Do

- Grow your own tomatoes and basil.

- Expect many visits from extended family.

- Learn to cook.

- Expect to have your balls broken.

- Expect to get married in a Catholic Church.

Don't

- Buy sauce in a jar.

- Expect your house to be quiet.

- Cook for less than 10 people when only three show up to eat.

- Take it personal.

- Expect your spouse to go to church except during holidays, weddings, and funerals.

CHAPTER SEVEN

Our Major Holidays

Holidays often go with family, and since family is important, we got a lot of respect for certain holidays. Many are religious, but it's not necessarily all about the religious part. Oh, sure, your Aunt Nina or Grandma make a big deal about Easter and Christmas Mass, but it's all about the family get-together.

Lent and Good Friday

Lent began on a Sunday in the 600s. Everyone decided to make themselves miserable because Jesus suffered for 40 days, so why can't you? The Pope moved it to a Wednesday because Ash Sunday didn't sound as good. Back then, they did real fasting, but people were like, "Yo, Pope! What kinda holiday has no food, huh?" By the 800s, you were allowed to eat after 3 p.m., then by the 1400s, you could eat after noon. It was okay to eat fish as long as you gave up meat. In 1966, the Catholic Church limited the days of fast to just Ash Wednesday and Good Friday. Who knows how relaxed the rules will be by 2066? Maybe all you have to do is not chew gum or abstain from eating a penguin.

Another thing: The Church wants you to give up something for Lent to do penance. (I can promise you, it won't be pasta. Do you want an Italian to starve to death?) It should be some kind of vice, but not something you're gonna easily fail at. You don't want to spend a lot of time in confession. The nuns will know. They got powers. The perfect thing to give up is something that will annoy you. Things like chocolate, drinking, gambling, banging your girl on the side—these are all good things to give up for Lent.

On top of that, you can't eat meat on Fridays. That's the Italian-American way of fasting, I guess. I mean, if you think we're going to stop eating everything, good luck with that! Technically, you gotta continue to do it through Holy Saturday until Easter Sunday.

Palm Sunday and Easter

Back in the day, palm branches symbolized a victory. That's why people threw them in front of Jesus when he came back to Jerusalem. You'd think they'd give Jesus something a little nicer. Like a house or a horse or something, but people were poor back then. I'm sure, if there were any Italians present, somebody's grandmother fed him.

Anyhow, on that day, Italians are probably gonna go to church and then have early Sunday dinner.

Then there's Easter. Easter Sunday combines family dinner with a holiday, so you'd better show up. Most people do, since they're irritable from all the vices they gave up and the lack of meat. I promise you, there will be plenty of sausage and braciole at that meal!

In Italy they say Christmas is for family, but you can spend Easter with anybody. This will probably be your first big invite to a family get-together if you're a Medigan, so pay attention.

Easter started out as a pagan holiday, probably involving a lot of rabbits, chocolate, and discount mattress sales. Obviously, it's all about Jesus coming back from the dead. Again, if they had given him a horse instead of palms, maybe the Romans wouldn't have caught 'em. Just sayin'. Anyhow, on that day, Italians are probably gonna go to church and then have early Sunday dinner. You see the pattern here?

But there is a difference. Easter is more fancy. We got special food and everything.

Italians invented an Easter bread called *scarcella*. This is a loaf of braided sweet bread with an Easter egg in it. The bigger the loaf, the more eggs it tends to have. For dinner, you are probably going to have some ham pie. This is a savory pie with ricotta cheese, ham, egg, mozzarella, salami, prosciutto, and Parmesan cheese. Look it up online and make yourself one. It don't taste like any Italian food you know, mainly because there ain't no red sauce on it, but it's one of the most Italian and delicious things you can eat.

Then there's the traditional calzone. Not that frozen crap you get in the box, and not mozzarella and red sauce—that's a pizza turnover. A traditional calzone has ricotta, no red sauce, plus sausage or ham, mozzarella, Romano, and various other cheeses and spices.

You might also get some lamb. That might be roasted lamb chops, or *capuzzelle di agnello*, otherwise known as roasted lamb's head! It's good, don't worry. Somebody probably just made it to mess with you. Imagine your reaction when they serve you a head!

Mother's Day

You miss Mother's Day, you might as well not show up for Sunday dinner. She does all that cooking for you, you bet your ass you're gonna come up with some flowers or something good for Ma. And while you're at it, better do something for your grandma, too. Plus any other female relatives that are mothers.

Trust me, you don't want to start doing all the cooking. And keep in mind, they usually do the cleanup afterward, too. So if you don't want to work all day during the other holidays, make sure you mark your calendar.

Memorial Day

Italians will use almost any excuse to throw a party and invite the relatives. Memorial Day, the start of summer, has definitely been added to that list. Sure, we do hamburgers and hot dogs, but we also do sweet and hot Italian sausage on the grill. Plus, we usually bring better bread. Nothin' in plastic, c'mon.

Father's Day

Now Italian dads are a little more low-key by appearances, but they demand respect, and they deserve it. You don't have to make as big a fuss as you do with Ma, but you gotta make the effort. Just like your ma is worried about everyone having enough to eat, your father is going to be worried about the family getting together. Showing up is almost enough, but ya know, get him something nice: a Frank Sinatra CD, a Blu-ray of *The Godfather I* and *II*, something he needs for making wine—you know, father stuff.

Italian Festivals

According to the Sons of Italy, the oldest Italian-American fraternal order in the US, there are 361 Italian festivals held across the country every year. That's a lot of guys standin' around going, "Oh! Nice festival!" Most of them happen in the summer or when the weather's nice or when the local church needs some new pews. We'd need a whole new book to cover all of them, but know that most happen in the Northeast, with New York and New Jersey leading the pack with 61 and 50 festivals, respectively.

The oldest is held in Hammonton, New Jersey. In 2017, the 142nd annual Our Lady of Mt. Carmel Festival was held from July 11 to 16. The festival was established in 1875 by grateful Italian immigrants. Antonio Capelli and some of the other faithful prayed in front of a painting of the Virgin Mary, thanking her for their good fortune. The festival was their way of giving back. Little did they know that they would keep carnival ride operators and skee ball alley rental places in business for years to come.

The feast week consists of plenty of food (served by volunteers of the Our Lady of Mt. Carmel Society). There's also carnival rides, games, singers, and other entertainment. The main event, however, is the procession of the saints. Just like in Italy, the saint procession starts at the church, and statues of the saints are carried (or in this case, rolled) out. The faithful pin money, along with their prayers, onto the saints. Marching bands, the Sons of Italy, the Italian-American Club, and other local organizations march and participate.

If Italian festivals aren't holidays, I don't know what is.

Labor Day

Again, not a particularly Italian holiday, but a good excuse to throw a party. It's the traditional end of summer, so you crack open the grill one last time, tell the cousins to come over, and make a ridiculous amount of food. Summer is the time for crabs and clams, which Italians love. Italy has a lot of coast, and seafood has always been a staple of Italian food. You gotta love seafood to eat scungilli and *baccala*.

....

baccala. an Italian fish dish made from salted cod, which must be soaked for days.

You eat that baccala! I had to soak that fuckin' fish for two days!

....

Columbus Day

All right, now everybody just calm down, okay? People get up in arms about Columbus. But if he hadn't mapped the route to America, half of the country would still be sittin' somewhere in Europe with bad teeth and no internet. Regardless of where you stand, there's some interesting history here to discuss.

What you gotta understand about Columbus Day is that Columbus was Italian, and the day is a symbol of acceptance of Italians in the United States. It became a day to celebrate our heritage. As early as October 12, 1866, Italians were celebrating Columbus in New York City. At that time, we were the "weird" immigrants with crazy exotic foods and traditions. We wanted to be accepted as Americans.

Angelo Noce was one of these Italians. He lived in an Italian community in Denver and lobbied a Hispanic state senator to make Columbus Day an official holiday. In 1907, that state senator, Casimio Barela, sponsored the bill and in 1909, Denver held its first

Columbus Day parade. Other states started adopting the holiday, because who don't want a day off from work, right? By the time Angelo passed in 1922, 35 states had the holiday. These days, only Hawaii, Alaska, Oregon, South Dakota, and Vermont don't recognize Columbus Day.

Christmas

For Italians, Christmas has it all. Food, family, presents, candy, special bread, special food, church, and probably some pointless arguments over decorations, because who puts Christmas lights on a wooden deer, Marie? It's supposed to be a tree or your house or nothin'!

Anyhow, this is the most important family dinner of the year. All the relatives come out for it, even the ones that only make it to weddings and funerals. A traditional Italian dinner is the Feast of the Seven Fishes. The meal dates back to Roman times when ancient Catholics would abstain from eating meat and dairy during holidays. In the early 1900s, Italian-Americans made the tradition popular again.

The feast actually happens on Christmas Eve, so you're supposed to eat light, thus the fish. But, ya know, we Italians laugh when someone says they're gonna eat light at a family dinner.

The seven fishes can vary, according to family tastes. Technically any fish is fine, but the traditional seven fishes usually include baccala, deep fried smelts (little cooked fishes you just pick up and eat), scungilli salad (sliced conch mixed with spices and olives), *galamad* (what you would call calamari: fried squid, or sometimes squid in a salad), pasta with a seafood sauce (clams, anchovy, crabs or tuna), clams (maybe clams casino, or just some steamed clams), and then something everyone likes, like shrimp. There's a bunch of other choices, but it depends on each particular Italian family. I'd be surprised if you didn't get at least four of these at a feast.

Besides the usual amazing bread at an Italian meal, there's likely to be panettone. It kinda tastes like a fruitcake had a baby with a nice light loaf of bread. There might also be some *sfogliatelle* (Italian for "puffs") or clamshell, which is like a light, filo dough pastry with almond or ricotta filling. Some families have *struffoli* or *zapes*. Both are fried dough balls, but the former is small and sweet, and the latter could be sweet or might have anchovy in it. Big surprise if you get those mixed up! Or, you could go totally Italian classic dessert with some cannoli or tiramisu. No matter how you go, if you eat with an Italian family at Christmas, wear loose pants.

CHAPTER EIGHT

Gambling and Other Italian Religious Practices

Italians like to gamble, although not to excess. The Mafia (if it existed) considers gambling addicts or degenerate gamblers the lowest form of life. Never bet more than you can lose or explain to your wife.

Gambling Stats

In the 1980s, Mafia families counted on 60 percent of their income from gambling, which was illegal in most states. It was definitely illegal in New York and New Jersey, where many Italians lived. Then, legalized gambling in Atlantic City and elsewhere opened the floodgates. Organized crime families were eventually driven out of Atlantic City casinos by the corporations. (Mobsters had to worry about jail or getting killed. Guys in corporate businesses, they would just get fired and replaced.)

According to a recent study on gambling, Americans lost $116.9 billion dollars at the tables in 2016. That's more than in any other country. Italy came in fourth, with $19 billion. About half those losses in the US were from legal casinos, but in Italy, about half were from non-casino gambling machines. The US ranks its loss per resident per year at about $450 per person, while Italy is only around $380 per resident.

Broken down by state, New York ranks seventh and New Jersey ranks third. Combine both states and they only rank behind Nevada. Considering that New Jersey only has 23 casinos and New York has 22, ranking 16th and 17th in the number of casinos by state, this means a lot of gambling is happening.

Basically, if there's a card game to be found, there's always going to be an Italian or two to ante in.

Catholic Stats

You might consider Italy a mostly Catholic country, but you'd be wrong. A 2016 poll placed the number of Italians that call themselves Catholic only at 50 percent, with the next biggest number being atheists, at 20 percent. Don't tell Nana!

The demographics of Catholics are changing in the United States, where around 22 percent of the population considers themselves Catholic. That's around 71 million Catholics, give or take. There are around 17 million Italian-Americans, and most of them are Catholic, or were, meaning that there are probably somewhere between 5 and 17 million Italian-American Catholics. Judging by what's going on in Italy, you could probably ball park it around 8.5 or 9 million. There's lots of lapsed Catholics out there, but when they get old, they come running back. You don't wanna die and find out you're wrong. You'll look like an asshole in front of Jesus!

Growing Up Catholic

It starts when you get baptized as a baby. Right then, you get a set a godparents, which is like having a bonus aunt and uncle. As if you didn't have enough relatives, right?

Most Italians grow up Catholic. This usually means going to a Catholic school, wearing the uniform, learning the sacraments, and getting your hand whacked by an angry nun if you step out of line. Sure, people dump on the Catholic Church these days (and they have a lot to answer for), but the teachers weren't just trying to teach reading, writing, and math. They were also trying to teach you a set of values.

Your First Communion is a big event and yeah, it's another excuse to throw a party. After spending weeks studying, you finally get to be a real member of a church. From there, it's usually a downhill slide until you start to wonder, "Jesus Christ, how many times do I gotta fuckin' kneel during a church service? Did God hate seats?"

Finally, the next big event is when you turn 18 and get a driver's license and a car. Then you can finally start making excuses to your mother why you weren't in church on Sunday. Those nuns can't do nothin' after that!

But then later, when you go to get married, your parents are going to want you to get married to a Catholic in a Catholic Church. Then you have kids and you gotta make 'em go to church, so you'll find yourself back in a pew soon enough. At least this way, your nana won't yell at you during Sunday dinner.

CHAPTER NINE

Sinatra and Other Famous Italians

This is the chapter that seals the deal. Here, you're gonna learn all about the famous Italians that changed history and made the world a better place. (Except maybe for two or three.) Really makes you think. Without Italians, where would the world be? Probably quiet and bland.

Frank Sinatra

Let's face it, Frank Sinatra was just about the coolest guy to walk God's green Earth. This was a man who looked naked without a glass Scotch and a cigarette in his hand. (The rest of the Rat Pack was no exception, and included fellow Italian, Dean Martin.) Sinatra sold over 150 million records worldwide, and his music continues to please anyone who has ever walked into an Italian restaurant. He also won an Academy Award, a Golden Globe, 11 Grammys, the Presidential Medal of Freedom, and the Congressional Gold Medal.

But probably the greatest thing Frank was known for, other than his singing and his crazy lifestyle, was his generosity. Not only did he throw his money around to friends and family that needed it, he used his clout as one of the most famous guys of his day to speak out against racism. And he didn't just speak out when it was popular to do so: As far back as 1945, he was speaking up. He also got involved with politics and helped elect John F. Kennedy, among others. These days, a famous singer can't say nothin' about no one without getting blasted in the press. Frank not only had principles, he had the balls to stick by them when the going got tough, even at the risk of his own career.

Other Entertainers

Robert De Niro

One of the greatest Italian-American actors around, De Niro's portrayal of young Don Corleone in *The Godfather II* stands as one of the greatest pieces of cinema to date. *Taxi Driver* and his other films ain't too shabby neither, but did you know that De Niro wasn't the only creative guy in his family?

Robert De Niro Sr., who passed in 1993, was an abstract expressionist painter. The elder De Niro was pals with other creatives at the time, including poet Robert Duncan and writers Anais Nin, Henry Miller, and Tennessee Williams. Throughout the '50s he had solo exhibits, he traveled to France to paint the countryside in the '60s, and by the '70s and '80s, his paintings were exhibited all over the United States. His son's directorial debut, *A Bronx Tale*, was dedicated to De Niro Sr. So not only is De Niro a great actor, but he's a pretty damned good son by any measure. That's Italian family values in action.

Al Pacino

It's hard to talk about De Niro without mentioning Pacino. I mean, he was in *both Godfather* movies. *Dog Day Afternoon* and *Serpico* are among his classic portrayals. The guy's won an Academy Award, two Tony Awards, two Primetime Emmys, a British Academy Film Award, four Golden Globes, and lots more. You gotta be a real actor's actor to win awards for film, TV, and the stage. He's co-president of the Actors Studio with Ellen Burstyn and Harvey Keitel, and he's pretty much been averaging a movie or two every year for almost 50 years. Jesus, Al, take a vacation!

Joseph Barbera

You ever see a cartoon? Chances are it was either invented by or greatly influenced by Joe Barbera of Hanna-Barbera Productions. Among the shows Joe co-produced were *The Quick Draw McGraw Show*, *Jonny Quest*, *The Magilla Gorilla Show*, *Scooby-Doo*, the *Super Friends*, and *The Smurfs*. But his most famous cartoon was the one he created with Hanna, *Tom and Jerry*. Criticized as too violent, it featured a never-ending battle between a cat and mouse. *The Simpsons* continue to pay homage to it under the parody name, "Itchy and Scratchy."

So next time someone tries to drop an anvil on your head, you'll know who to thank.

Madonna

She is the best-selling female recording artist of all time and has sold 300 million records worldwide. For almost two decades, she not only defined music, but also fashion. Every girl wanted to be Madonna in the '80s.

Born Madonna Louise Ciccone, her parents were Catholic. (No big surprise with a name like that!) And anyone that's seen her videos, especially "Like a Prayer," can see how Catholicism influenced her. The Pope actually encouraged fans to boycott her in Italy, not that it worked.

And sure, she's done some weird shit over the years, but what entertainer hasn't? Britney Spears, Christina Aguilera, Pink, Miley Cyrus—they all owe a little something to the Material Girl. Plus, she still looks pretty hot for a woman in her 50s. C'mon, give her credit.

Nick LaRocca

Born Dominic James LaRocca, Nick was the leader of the Original Dixieland Jass Band; the band was the Frank Sinatra of its time. They made the first jazz recording in 1917, called *Livery Stable Blues*. But they also recorded *Tiger Rag*, one of the most recorded jazz classics of all time. For New Orleans jazz, 1917 was a huge year.

Gay Talese

An innovative best-selling author who has written 14 books, Gay was a *New York Times* reporter who developed the style of literary journalism. That's when you tell a factual news story, but in a more interesting and personal way. He wrote "Frank Sinatra Has a Cold," which was named "Best Story *Esquire* Ever Published." The son of an Italian immigrant tailor, he grew up Catholic and was born in Ocean City, New

Jersey. He's active in the National Italian-American Foundation and encourages Italian-Americans to become writers. Thanks, Gay!

Sports

Giuseppe Garibaldi

Bocce is plural for *boccia*, which is the Italian word for ball. Bocce goes back to the Egyptians, who played a version of the game as early as 5200 BC by throwing polished rocks. The Greeks picked it up, and then the Romans, and finally, the Italians. The Venetians and the Catholic Church frowned upon the game and banned it in 1576. Too much gambling was associated with the game. (Italians gambling on a sport, go figure!)

European royalty picked up on the game, but it wasn't nationalized as a sport until Giussepe helped out in 1896. The game is sorta like horseshoes, only with balls. You throw the little ball, or the pallino, then each team has four balls and tries to get them as close to the little ball as possible. You get one point for each ball that's closer to the pallino than your opponents, two points for a leaner.

Bocce came to America as the English version of the game, only it was called "bowls." George Washington had a bocce court at Mount Vernon. Even the father of our country wanted to be Italian. Who could blame him?

The World Bocce Championships started in Italy in 1947, and today the game is the third most popular sport in the world after soccer and golf. Umberto Granaglia is considered the Muhammad Ali and Michael Jordan of the sport. He won 13 World Championships, 12 European Championships, and 46 Italian Championships. Thanks to a bocce craze that hit California in 1989, more than 25 million Americans play the game—and not just old Italians. So hey, if you like to play with balls, get yourself a bocce set.

Mario Andretti

Mario's not just *a* race car driver; he's *the* race car driver. If Speed Racer were an actual guy, Mario could outdrive him. He was named driver of the year in 1967, 1978, and 1984. He was the first driver to win IndyCar races in four different decades. No American has won the Formula One race since Andretti won the 1978 Dutch Grand Prix. He's the only driver to win the Indy 500, Daytona 500, and Formula One World Championship. I mean, if you needed a pizza delivered, this guy could have it at your house before you were finished ordering the toppings!

Joe DiMaggio

Yep, the Yankee Clipper was born Giuseppe Paolo DiMaggio, and his brothers Dom and Vince were also major leaguers. This guy was one of the greatest baseball players of all time. He holds the MLB record for a 56-game hitting streak and earning three-time MVP, 13 All-Star seasons, 10 American League pennants, and nine World Series. C'mon, the man was a legend! (Plus, he got with Marilyn Monroe, the hottest woman to ever live.) Italians may not have invented baseball, but we had a guy who perfected it!

Joe Montana

I know, you hear "Montana" and you think the state, not Italian, but it's true. Joe's grandparents were Italian immigrants on his mother's side. He had four Super Bowl wins, got Super Bowl MVP three times, and had the most Super Bowl career passes without an interception. He's also responsible for "The Catch," considered one of the greatest plays in NFL history. Joe threw the game-winning touchdown against Dallas in the 1981 NFC Championship game with just 51 seconds left in the game.

Government

Antonin Scalia

Although he was appointed by Ronald Reagan back in the '80s, Scalia was the first Italian-American Supreme Court Justice. He was a devout Roman Catholic whose son entered the priesthood. Whether you agreed with his conservative politics or not, the man served for almost 30 years, right up until he died in 2016. (Don't worry, Samuel Alito is on the Supreme Court, and he's a goomba, too.) The guy definitely had an Italian attitude, not surprising for a guy who was born in New Jersey and grew up in Manhattan. And he was brave, too. The guy hunted with Dick Cheney. Then again, Cheney had more to be worried about if he ever decided to shoot Scalia in the face!

Joseph Petrosino

Joe joined the NYPD in 1883 and was the first Italian speaker on the force. He was friends with Theodore Roosevelt, who was on the Board of Police Commissioners in New York in 1895. Because Joe not only spoke Italian but several dialects, he was able to solve crimes other Medigan cops couldn't. He was eventually promoted to lieutenant in 1908 and was in charge of a special group of Italian-American detectives that investigated the Mafia. Even though the Mafia didn't exist, Joe felt it brought shame on law-abiding Italians and Italian-Americans.

Joe helped foil a blackmail scheme against a famous Italian opera singer, Enrico Caruso. He uncovered a plot by Italian anarchists to assassinate President McKinley. The Secret Service ignored him, despite being vouched for by Vice President Roosevelt. (Which is how Teddy got the top job, ironically.)

Unfortunately, this super-cop got assassinated on a secret mission to Palermo, Sicily, in 1909. Rumor has it, the hit was orchestrated by Cascio Ferro (a gangster Joe had helped arrest and deport) and by the Morello Crime Family, who survive as the Genovese Crime Family to this day.

Nancy Pelosi

Being in Congress is impressive enough, but being the first woman in US history to be Speaker of the House, that's big. Technically, she is the highest ranking female politician ever in US history, and she did all that while raising five kids! Nancy's mother, Annunciata Lombardi, was born in Campobasso, Italy, and her father was Thomas D'Alesandro III, a democratic representative from Maryland. She went to an all-girl Catholic school and Trinity College, a Catholic college. If anyone has got a shot at being the first Italian president, it's definitely Nancy. Whether you agree with her politics or not, her Italian credentials are impeccable!

Francis Barretto Spinola

A New Yorker through and through, Francis became the first Italian-American elected to Congress in 1887. But that was the least crazy job he had! In the 1850s, he joined the secret police that kept the peace during New York City's gang days. We're talking *Gangs of New York* kind of gangs. He was an alderman, New York State assemblyman, New York senator, and commissioner of New York Harbor. And during the Civil War, he was a Union brigadier general! He commanded four regiments called Spinola's Empire Brigade. After the war, he was a banker, an insurance agent, and then a member of Congress, as well as being a huge figure in the Italian-American community in New York. His funeral was at Immaculate

Conception Church in 1891, so you know he was Catholic, no question. His estate was valued at over a million dollars. What a life! A true paisan in every sense of the word.

Inventors

Eddie Arcaro

Anyone that knows the sport of horse racing knows Eddie. He's the most winning jockey in history, and was the only jockey to win the Triple Crown twice! He also helped established the Jockey's Guild, a professional organization for jockeys. Unfortunately, the organization went belly-up in 2007. After he retired in '62, he become a spokesman for Buick, and like all good Italian athletes, he opened his own Italian restaurant. He passed in 1997 and is immortalized in the American Thoroughbred Horse Racing Hall of Fame. What a shame. I'll bet he had some good betting tips.

Jacuzzi and Brothers

Did you ever wonder who invented the hot tub? Technically, it goes back to prehistoric times when people would put hot stones in the bath to heat up the water, or when they'd just fall into a hot spring. The Japanese were big on hot tubs starting in the 8th century, and of course, the ancient Romans like a good bath, too. But without bubbles, it's bullshit.

Enter the Jacuzzi Brothers. Giocondo Jacuzzi and his brothers started a business to build airplanes and propellers back in 1915, but they eventually figured out that you could blow bubbles in a bath tub. Originally, they were into something called "hydrotherapy," but then in the '70s someone figured out that it would be great to bang someone in the tub with the bubbles at the same time. Suddenly, everyone in the '70s was getting nude in the tub together. Hey, I'm not saying Italians invented swingers, but we helped.

Antonio Meucci

Who invented the telephone? Some Medigan named Alexander Graham Bell, right? Wrong! Antonio

Meucci invented the telephone in 1856 to talk to his wife while she was in bed, suffering from an illness. (See? Italians always doing something for the family!) Unfortunately, Meucci had some money problems and he didn't get a patent ready until 1871. He even invented the name and called his company the Telettrofono Company. Long story short, there was a trial about the patent with Bell's company, and Meucci got robbed (depending on who you ask). In 2002, United States Representative Vito Fossella (also Italian) helped pass a bill recognizing Meucci's contribution to the making of the telephone. Fat lot of good it did the poor bastard—Meucci died before the trial about the patent was even over.

Guglielmo Marconi

Everyone knows Marconi invented the radio. He also co-won the 1909 Nobel Prize in physics. Thanks to Marconi, the guys on the Titanic were able to radio for help. So while a lot of people died, they might've *all* died if not for Guglielmo's most recent invention. Marconi was a senator in the Italian Senate in 1914, but he fell into the wrong crowd and joined the

Italian Fascist Party in 1923. He died in 1937, hope-fully regretting his political affiliation. For the first time in history, radio stations observed a moment of silence for his passing. Hey, but if it weren't for him, there'd be nothin' but radio silence.

Scipione Riva-Rocci

An Italian doctor from Almese, Italy, this is the guy that invented that blood pressure cuff doctors use today. Scipione, being the good guy he was, refused to patent his invention and didn't make a dime off of it! He let famous doctor, Harvey Cushing, take it to America, improve it, and spread it around. What doctor do you know that doesn't have one of these? One of the most commonly used and important pieces of medical equipment, and the good doctor just wanted it out there to help people.

Charles Ponzi

Italians invent so many things, we're bound to invent some bad things. You ever hear of a Ponzi scheme? It was invented by an Italian. In the early 1920s, Chuck was the first guy to promise his clients 50 percent profit in 45 days or 100 percent profit in 90 days. Needless to say, he used the money from later investors to pay the earliest investors, swindling people to the tune of $20 mil. And that was in 1920 dollars! But Ponzi's scheme collapsed and he went to prison, losing everything. He died penniless in Brazil in 1949.

Frank Zamboni

Frank and his brother Lawrence ran an ice block business in Los Angeles. They opened the Iceland skating rink in 1940. In 1946, Frank patented a way to keep the rink ice from getting rippled, but it still took 90 minutes, a tractor, and a team of guys to resurface the rink after people were done using it. The inventive Italian created the machine that bears his family name and made the job easy. Thanks to Frank, hockey games can get back to guys wailing on each other that much quicker.

Lorenzo del Riccio

Lorenzo was an Italian immigrant working at Paramount Pictures in Los Angeles as a motion picture engineer. He invented the photo finish for horse racing. It was first used at Bing Crosby's Del Mar Turf Club in 1937. Although now the racetrack uses digital photos, Lorenzo's invention was an important innovation at the time. How else you think you could see if a horse wins by a nose? If anyone was going to improve gambling at the track, it would have to be an Italian.

Enrico Fermi

You like electricity in your house? Well, you can thank Enrico Fermi, the creator of the nuclear reactor. He also worked on the Manhattan Project and is known as the Architect of the Atomic Bomb. In 1938, Fermi fled Italy because of Il Douchebag to save his Jewish wife from the Fascists. He won the Nobel Prize in Physics in 1938 and built the first nuclear reactor in 1942. He served with J. Robert Oppenheimer on the Atomic Energy Commission. Fermi is so famous in the scientific community he has a slew of awards and institutions named after him. He even has his own element on the periodical table: fermium!

And the Rest

Wally Schirra

Wally was the first Italian-American in space. It's a good thing we got a paisan up there early; you don't want the Medigans facing aliens alone. Wally was the first astronaut to go into space three times, and the only person to fly in the Mercury, Gemini, and Apollo programs. Old-timers might remember him as being Walter Cronkite's co-anchor for all seven moon landings. Later, he was hired as the spokesman for Actifed, the same cold medicine he took on the Apollo missions. After he passed in 2007, he was cremated and they had a burial-at-sea for his ashes on the *USS Ronald Reagan*; a fitting end for a Navy pilot that had done it all.

Biaggio Paternostro

Biaggio makes Hollywood stars. Not the ones that appear in movies, but the ones on the Hollywood Walk of Fame! The Paternostro family has been making the stars for over 50 years, with Biaggio's grandson, David, currently in charge of things. The walk has over 2,600 stars with five categories: film, TV, radio, recordings, and live theater. Italians, we can't get away from construction. When you've been mixing cement since Roman times, I guess it's inevitable.

Famous Italians You Didn't Know Were Italian

There are lots of Italians that don't look Italian or have an Italian-sounding last name. Many of the entertainers change their names to make them easier to pronounce. Besides, you gotta use almost every freakin' vowel getting a name like De Napoliello on a marquee. For whatever reason, here now are some Italians you probably didn't know where Italian.

Alan Alda

That's right. Hawkeye from *M*A*S*H* is a paisan. His real name was Alphonso Joseph D'Abruzzo, and he was born in the Bronx. His dad, also an actor, called himself Robert Alda, but his real name was Alphonso Giuseppe Giovanni Roberto D'Abruzzo. Robert created his stage name by taking the first two letters of his first name and the first two letters of his last name. With his original name, they'd need a bigger screen for his credit!

F. Murray Abraham

Another great Italian actor, he was named Murray Abraham. His father was Syrian, but his mother was Italian. He added the "F" to his name to honor his dad, Fahrid. You probably remember him from movies like *Scarface* and the *Grand Budapest Hotel*, and from TV shows like *Homeland*.

Jay Leno

The famous comedian and former host of the *Tonight Show* had an Italian dad. Jay's full name is James Douglas Muir Leno. His grandparents on his father's side were immigrants from Flumeri, Italy. However, there is a place called Leno, Italy, far to the north, east of Milan. It may be that Jay's ancestors emigrated south before coming to America with their large chins.

Frank Zappa

Contrary to popular rumor, Frank wasn't the son of TV's Mr. Green Jeans on *Captain Kangaroo*. Frank Vincent Zappa was the son of Francis Vincent Zappa, a scientist. He grew up in a household where his grandparents spoke Italian. Both of his parents had Sicilian ancestry, so it's no wonder that the late great musician did his own thing in music despite what everyone else was doin'.

Steven Tyler

The lead singer of Aerosmith was born Steven Victor Tallarico in Manhattan. Giovanni, his paternal grandfather, was from Cotronei, an area in Calabria, Italy. Tyler formed Aerosmith with lead guitarist and fellow goomba, Anthony Joseph Pereira, otherwise known as Joe Perry. Just more evidence that Italians know how to rock.

Charles Atlas

A world-renowned bodybuilder and exercise guru with that kind of name? It had to be made up. What you probably didn't know was that he was born Angelo Siciliano. That's probably one of the most Italian names you can have. Charles was born in Acri,

Italy, in Calabria. He was the original guy that got sand kicked in his face at the beach, then muscled up to kick some ass!

Alicia Keys

Another New Yorker, she was born Alicia Augello Cook in Manhattan. Her dad was African American and her mother was of Sicilian descent. Her mother's last name was Augello, which in Italian is a nickname for a small, birdlike person. Alicia sings like a songbird, that's for sure. You don't win 15 Grammys and 17 NAACP Image Awards without being super talented.

The Jonas Brothers

All three of the brothers are Italians from New Jersey. They probably should've called themselves the Jonas Crew.

Hulk Hogan

The Hulkster was born Terry Eugene Bollea, son of Pietro Bollea. Just another Italian you don't want to mess with.

Weird Al Yankovic

Yep, Weird Al's mom is Italian and had the maiden name of Vivalda. In Latin, this last name means "brave in battle."

Lady Gaga

Now you knew this isn't her real name, but did you know it's Stefani Joanne Angelina Germanotta? She's from the Upper East Side of Manhattan and was raised Catholic. She went to the Convent of the

Sacred Heart, an all-girl, private Catholic school. She's now one of the best-selling musicians of all time, with 27 million albums and 146 million songs sold. Not bad, Stefani.

Jenna Jameson

Arguably the world's most famous porn star, she was born Jenna Marie Massoli and was raised Catholic. Ya gotta wonder if the nuns that taught her got fired, or at least retrained.

Jimmy Kimmel

James Christian Kimmel was born in Brooklyn. His mother was Italian with the maiden name Iacono. He was raised Catholic and was an altar boy. His uncle, Frank Potenza, made appearances on the Jimmy Kimmel Show until he passed in 2011. His cousin, Sal

Iacono, is a writer and performer on the show. Good job keepin' it in the family, Jimmy.

Kelly Ripa

The morning talk show host is a Jersey girl and was raised Catholic. She was inducted into the New Jersey Hall of Fame in 2017. (As if people from New Jersey need to go to a hall to find out how famous she is!)

And the Rest...

We Italians are everywhere, but just to wrap this up, more famous Italians you many not know are Italian include Sonny Bono, Rachel Ray (which you probably knew), singer Chris Isaak, famed golfer Fred Couples (whose father changed the family name from Coppola), Nikki Sixx from Motley Crue, Mary Lou Retton (whose grandfather changed the family name from Rotunda), Steve Vai, Cyndi Lauper (and her friend,

Captain Lou Albano), comedian Chris Hardwick, John Cena, Joe Rogan, Gerard Way of My Chemical Romance, Megyn Kelly (formerly of Fox News), and former Chairman to the Joint Chiefs of Staff, General Peter Pace, to name a few.

CHAPTER ELEVEN

Talk Like a Paisan: A Handy Glossario of Italian Words

Like a lot of immigrants, Italians mix language from the Old Country with phrases and words from their new homeland. A lot of these words you'll hear when an Italian is excited or angry. Depending on what generation walked off the boat, they'll use some of the words more or less.

agita. heartburn or acid indigestion; usually associated with some kind of bad or frustrating news.

I wish you'd shut your dog up! He's giving me agita!

antipasto. see page 75.

baccala. see page 120.

braciole. see page 73.

brugad. slang for *borgata*, meaning crime family.
Don't mess with that guy. He's a member of a brugad.

butana. see page 65.

capeche. see page 8.

chooch. dumbass, moron, idiot.
Michael, don't be chooch. Give your sister her car back.

escarole. see page 90.

fangool. go fuck yourself or fuck you; probably a modified version of the Italian word *vaffanculo*.
Fangool! And never disrespect my Nana's lasagna again!

gabbadost. see page 76.

gabbagool. slang for *capicola*, a deli meat made from pork shoulder.
Stunad! How you gonna make antipasto without some gabbagool, huh?

gavone. see page 7.

goomba. see page 17

gumad. slang for the Italian word *cumare*, meaning girl on the side or mistress.

Joseph's wife found out about his gumad and now he's getting divorced.

jabonee or jaboney. derogatory word used by some Italian-Americans for immigrant Italians; not to be confused with "jabroni," which is a wrestling term that only sounds Italian.

You can't hire that jabonee! He don't speak no English good!

jamook. moron, idiot, loser.

I got scratches all over my car because that jamook at the car wash didn't know what he was doin'!

made guy. see page 87.

Madonn'. see page 21.

Mafia. Sicilian organized crime.

> *The Mafia don't exist.*

mamaluke. dummy, idiot, moron; may have originated from the Arab word *mamluk*, meaning slave solider.

> *Instead of helping his father at work, Jake went home and watched* Game of Thrones! *What is wrong with that mamaluke?*

mannigott. short for *manicotti*, large pasta tubes usually filled with ricotta cheese.

> *You can't overcook the mannigott or the ricotta will just fall out when you serve it.*

Medigan. see page 9.

oobatz. see page 22.

paisan. see page 63.

pasta-vazool. *pasta fagioli*, a mixture of pasta, beans, and sometimes chicken.

> *Hey, this is good pasta-vazool! You should open a restaurant!*

prochute. short for prosciutto, sometimes pro-nounced "brochute;" an Italian ham you'll find in most delis.

This isn't an Italian hoagie without prochute!

salut. short for *salute*, which basically means "cheers" when drinking.

Thanks for bringing your homemade wine to the card game, Sal. Salut.

schifozz. see page 68.

scungilli. see page 8.

stugatz/stoogotts. slang for the Italian words *stu cazz*, meaning "the dick"; in Italian-American slang, it usually refers to a person who is annoying.

I tell you, Paulie, stugatz over here is disrespecting us!

stunad. see page 9.

vaffanculo. see page 65.

Vespa. see page 30.

vig. short for "vigorish," a percentage paid to bookies by the gamblers.

What's the vig on the Philadelphia/Dallas game?

whacked. see page 23.

CHAPTER TWELVE

Great Moments in Italian History

40 million years ago: The Alps formed. Ski lift lines begin.

850,000 years ago: First hominids arrive in Italy. They immediately start talking more with their hands.

April 21, 753 BC: Romulus and Remus establish Rome and immediately start creating buildings whose images would later appear on Italian restaurant walls.

April 1, 30 AD: Saint Peter technically becomes the first pope, but the Catholic Church was just starting out, so he didn't have a lot of fancy jewels and clothes yet.

March 15, 44 AD: Julius Caesar gets whacked after a bunch of the Roman senators return from a trip to the bathroom with knives.

79 AD: Mount Vesuvius covers the Roman city of Pompeii, freezing almost everyone in the town in volcanic dust and lava. Hundreds of years later, cable TV channels would do specials on how many whore houses were in the town.

117 AD–ca. 284 AD: Rome hits its peak, with four to five million citizens, around three million square miles of territory, and more bread stores than you've ever seen.

199: Natalius, the first Anti-Pope of Rome, is elected. This wasn't an "evil" pope, just a pope that got elected as a rival to the actual pope. There was a lot of division in the church over the centuries, and Anti-Popes were elected for centuries alongside regular popes. That's twice as many pope-mobiles!

August 24, 410: Visigoths sack Rome. King Alaric I leads the barbarians and ends Rome's 800-year stretch without falling to a foreign enemy. Oh, well.

It was a good run. Alaric dies the same year, probably because someone gave him the evil eye. (The evil eye is a curse that someone, usually an old woman, would put on you. Wearing a *cornicello*, or a "little horn," wards off the evil eye. That's why Italians wear the horn—no, it's not a chili pepper.)

March 25, 421: At noon on that day, Venice was established to escape the hordes of barbarians that were tearing up the Roman countryside. Eventually, someone pointed out they were standing in waist-deep water, and they decided to build a city so that their children might one day have dry shoes.

476: Flavius Odoacer becomes the first King of Italy, but is later killed by the indirect actions of the Roman Emperor that gave him the job. Technically, the first Italian to get whacked.

June 22, 816: First Italian Pope elected to office: Stephen IV, who is sometimes called Stephen V, probably because of some mix-up with paperwork. There were so many popes.

897: Pope Stephen VI has his predecessor, Pope Formosus, dug up, dressed in a pope outfit, and put on trial. Needless to say, it didn't go well for the dead guy. What did they give him, a dead lawyer to defend himself?

997: The word "pizza" first appears. Immediately, someone begins sketching an Italian chef holding one up in the air with one hand.

1053: The Great Schism in the Catholic Church begins. Eastern Orthodox Church–goers go their own way. The Catholics laugh and say, "Being Catholic will always be more popular." Ya know, unless something really bad happens. But what are the odds of that?

1271: Marco Polo begins his famous journey and tells his wife he's just going out for cigarettes.

Easter Day, 1282: Some French guy says the wrong thing to a Sicilian woman, creating the Sicilian Vespers, who then drive the French out of Sicily. May or may not have been the prototype for the Mafia, which don't exist.

1295: Marco Polo returns, reporting that there's no good bread outside of Italy.

July 20, 1304: Francesco Petrarca, a.k.a. Petrarch, is born. He is considered one of the first humanists. His very influential poetry and writing made historians name him "The Father of the Renaissance." Basically, he was the Italian equivalent of that guy that plays guitar in your dorm, smokes weed, and then gets all deep.

1320: Dante Alighieri finishes writing the *Divine Comedy*. It's considered one of the greatest works in Italian and world literature. Dante passes a year later, unable to reap the massive rewards that poets normally get for their work.

ca. 1420: The Italian Renaissance starts. Italians tell everyone in Europe to stop fuckin' around. Over the next few centuries, there is a cultural and scientific explosion like humanity has never seen before.

1449: The last Anti-Pope, Felix V, retires from office to further the political ambitions of his children. Nothin' but regular popes from here on.

1492: Columbus reaches North America, earning everyone a free Monday off in October and encouraging debates in the future. 1495. Leonardo DaVinci paints "The Last Supper," giving every Italian grandmother in the world something to hang on the wall in the kitchen.

May 14, 1501: Amerigo Vespucci leaves to discover South America and steal the naming rights, which is why we're not called "The United States of Columbia."

1513: Niccolò Machiavelli writes *The Prince*, stating, amongst other concepts, "the ends justifies the means," giving politicians everywhere justification for acting like assholes.

1514: Leonardo DaVinci paints the "Mona Lisa," creating the easiest trivia question known to man and giving Nat King Cole something to sing about.

1522: The tomato arrives in Italy. Italian grandmothers everywhere immediately begin cooking amazing sauce.

April 17, 1524: Giovanni da Verrazzano, an Italian explorer, becomes the first Italian to map New York Harbor and visit the island of Manhattan. After getting caught in traffic and eating a slice, he leaves. He tells the locals to make sure to spell his name right if they ever name a bridge after him.

1599: Monks run out of cemetery plots in Palermo and start building catacombs that would be used all the way up until the 1920s. The Catacombs of Palermo are still creepy as shit.

July 1633: Galileo tells the Inquisition to go fuck themselves despite the threat of torture. He spends the rest of his life under house arrest writing some of his best work anyway.

1664: *Gazzetta di Mantova* is established in Mantua, Italy, and is still published today. It's one of the oldest daily Italian newspapers in existence.

1750: *The Beggar's Opera* becomes the first Italian opera to be performed in America in New York. Tickets were 50 cents, or like $500 apiece today. People still can't get tickets.

1776: Pascal DeAngelis joins the New York State Militia during the outbreak of the American Revolution. He's Italian and only 13 years old. He serves until the war ends in 1783. Some balls on this kid!

August 2, 1776: The Declaration of Independence is signed and at least two of the signers are Italian: William Paca of Maryland, and Caesar Rodney of Delaware. These two goombas told the Brits they could go screw with that tea tax.

1778: Phillip Mazzei goes to the Duke of Tuscany to borrow money to help the Founding Fathers pay for the Revolutionary War. Mazzei assures the duke that if he doesn't pony up, the Brits will win, and instead of good Italian restaurants in Manhattan, it'll be nothin' but fish and chips.

1848: First commercial pasta plant in the United States opens in Brooklyn.

1853: Father Eugenio Barsanti and Felice Matteucci invent the first internal combustion engine. Later that year, their mechanic charges them $400 for a bunch of bullshit they probably didn't need.

1856: Father Giovanni Caselli invents the pantele-graph, a precursor to the fax machine. Almost immediately, he begins receiving Chinese food menus and offers for low mortgage rates.

March 17, 1861: Victor Emanuel II is crowned King of a united Italy. Italians finally agree to stop fighting with each other and just yell all the time.

June 17, 1863: Luigi Palma di Cesnola becomes the first Italian awarded the Medal of Honor. It was awarded for his bravery leading the Fourth New York Cavalry to take a hillside battery. He not only did that, but also captured 100 Confederates, got stabbed, got shot, and survived the war. See? You don't mess with an Italian in wartime.

October 1867: Giuseppina Morlacchi, an Italian balle-rina, debuts in New York and introduces the popular French dance, the can-can, to American audiences. Her legs were insured for $100,000.

May 1, 1886: Ristorante Fior d'Italia opens in San Fran-cisco. Open almost continuously since that time, it's the oldest Italian restaurant in America. Ralph's, in South Philly, has been continuously open since 1900.

1871: Rome becomes the Italian capital, marking the complete reunification of Italy as a kingdom and country. Shortly after, the first Italian uses the phrase "What are you lookin' at?"

June 26, 1876: Giovanni Martino becomes the only member of Custer's company to survive The Battle of the Little Big Horn. One look at Giovanni and the Indians were like, "Uh-uh. No. We're not messin' with that guy."

1887: Francis B. Sinola becomes the first Italian-American elected to the House of Representatives. Sadly, he served too late to outlaw sauce in a jar.

March 14, 1891: Eleven Italians are lynched in New Orleans; 50 other lynchings of Italians would occur between 1890 and 1920.

January 1, 1892: The first station at Ellis Island opens. A lot of Italian immigrants would pass through its doors looking for a better life in America, along with some decent bread.

July 29, 1900: An Italian immigrant who moved to Patterson, New Jersey, becomes an anarchist. He returns to Italy and assassinates King Umberto I. The assassin is found dead in his cell, a victim of "suicide." Yeah, right!

October 17, 1904: Amadeo Giannini founds the Bank of Italy in San Francisco to help immigrants settling in the United States. He eventually merged it with another bank and it became Bank of America. See that? Italians practically invented banking!

June 22, 1905: Dr. Vincenzo Sellaro forms the Order of the Sons of Italy in America, giving Italian-Americans everywhere support and a place to play cards.

1906: Amadeo Obici and Mario Peruzzi start Planters Peanuts. Mr. Peanut is based on the drawings of a young schoolboy named Antonio Gentile, who entered a contest. Later, Obici paid for Antonio and his four siblings to go to college. Mr. Peanut is, therefore, very Italian. His first name is probably Vinny. Vinny Peanut. Yeah, that sounds right.

1908: *L'Italo-Americano*, a newspaper aimed at the Italian-American community, is established and still publishes today. In that newspaper, Marmaduke won't shut up!

July 26, 1908: The FBI is formed by Attorney General Charles Bonaparte (who was related to Napoleon, who was also Italian). So everyone remembers that Al Capone was Italian, but no one remembers that the FBI was started by one.

October 12, 1909: First official Columbus Day parade is held in Denver.

December 12, 1915: Frank Sinatra is born! Italians everywhere begin drinking more Scotch, smoking cigarettes, and wearing fedoras.

1920: The Piccirilli Brothers carve the Lincoln Memorial. This is just one of their many world-renowned marble sculptures, which also include the Tomb of the Unknown Soldier, carved 11 years later.

January 20, 1920: Federico Fellini is born. He would later become one of the most influential filmmakers of all time and give film nerds and Woody Allen something to talk about on dates.

November 1, 1920: Charles Ponzi pleads guilty to 86 counts of mail fraud for his Ponzi scheme, losing his investors over $20 million dollars. He is the inspiration for many generations of scumbags who insist they can double your money.

1927: Frank Borzage wins the first Academy Award for Best Directing. Everyone immediately complains that the movie that should've won didn't win.

July 1928: Al Capone moves to the Lexington Hotel in Chicago and builds a secret vault and leaves it empty, hoping that it will be opened sometime in the future by some gavone news reporter.

February 11, 1929: Vatican City is established to give the pope and his many hats a nice place to live.

May 1929: The Atlantic City Conference takes place. Every major crime figure in the USA prepares for the end of Prohibition. A few of these figures may or may not have been Italian.

1934: Fiorello H. La Guardia is elected the first Italian mayor of New York City. After making sweeping reforms, unifying the transit system, and smashing corruption in city government, all he asks is that someday his name be given to an airport with no subway stop, so you have to take a cab.

July 11, 1934: Giorgio Armani is born in a very slimming, black $2,000 suit. Everyone agrees the baby looks amazing.

1939: Italian serial killer Leonarda Cianciulli becomes convinced that the only way to save her son, who has just enlisted in the Italian Army in time for World War II, was to sacrifice humans. She murders three women and turns them into soap to hide the bodies. She gets 30 years in prison, giving a whole new meaning to saying "don't drop the soap."

January 1940: Carmen Infantino co-creates comic book superhero, The Flash, and has a huge impact on the comic book business as an artist and editor. That makes The Flash part Italian. Instead of red, white, and gold for his costume, it should've been red, white, and green.

April 25, 1940: Al Pacino is born. Afterward, the doctor slaps him and he says "Hoo-ha!" for the first time.

1942: 1,881 Italian immigrants are placed in Italian Internment Camps, while many more people of Japanese descent are similarly interned. Hundreds of thousands were required to be photographed and fingerprinted.

February 1942: The Italian-American Labor Council, formed by Luigi Antonini, demands that the blanket law against immigrants be lifted. Luigi works with antiwar and antifascist movements before the war and helps the Allies during the war. He eventually gets the majority of restrictions lifted for most Italians on Columbus Day, 1942. The Italians trapped in camps are only released after Italy surrenders a year later.

August 17, 1943: Robert De Niro is born. The doctor gets scared when the baby gives him a look.

April 28, 1945: Benito Mussolini and his mistress get popped, along with the rest of the assholes in his crew. They hang his fat ass from the gas station sign the next day.

1946: Frank Capra makes *It's a Wonderful Life* and goes on to become one of the most influential filmmakers in history. Frank is mostly known for his positive and wholesome movies. You can't get depressed during a Capra film.

May 6, 1946: Italy votes out the monarchy and becomes a republic. Now no one can officially say "yes" to the question, "What, you think you're better than me?"

1947: First Ferraris are built, giving hope to every rich guy with a small package.

1948: *Life with Luigi* begins on CBS Radio, featuring an Italian immigrant stereotype. The radio show lasts until 1953. A TV show starts in 1952 but is removed from the airwaves under pressure from the Italian-American community. Decades later, Luigi's brother Mario would make him second banana in his video game as punishment.

1950s: Lauren Bacall refers to Humphrey Bogart and his friends by saying "You look like a goddamned rat pack" after a drunken trip to Las Vegas. This becomes the nickname for the famous crew of crooners that include Frank Sinatra, Dean Martin, and Sammy Davis Jr.

1952: Lorenzo J. Ponza Jr. invents the first baseball pitching machine so people don't have to keep walking to the other side of the batting cage to pick up the ball.

1954: Anthony T. Rossi invents flash pasteurization so that people can have fresh-squeezed orange juice taste without making it from concentrate. He calls the juice Tropicana Pure Premium. Now every morning, you gotta thank Italians at breakfast.

April 27, 1956: Rocky Marciano retires from boxing as an undefeated heavyweight champion and is still considered one of the greatest boxers of all time.

1957: The Genovese Family hosts the next meeting of the Commission and it does not go well. Crime families realize that gangster-only parties are not a great idea.

1962: Albert R. Broccoli produces *Dr. No*, the first James Bond movie, and would be involved with 16 films of the franchise. C'mon, no character that cool could be created without the help of an Italian!

September 1964: Sergio Leone releases *A Fistful of Dollars*, starring Clint Eastwood. This establishes Eastwood as a movie star and Leone as the Father of Spaghetti Westerns.

1966–1967: Vince Lombardi leads the Green Bay Packers to two straight Super Bowls and five NFL Championships in seven years. He is considered by many to be the greatest football coach in history. The man never had a losing season as a head coach! Incredible! If they were gonna make a saint of football, it would be Vince.

1968: Tracksuits are invented. Some Italians immediately begin wearing them with gold chains and sleeveless t-shirts. Very few actually run track.

October 11, 1968: Apollo 7 is launched with Walter Schirra, who becomes the first man to travel to space three times and the only man to serve on the Mercury, Gemini, and Apollo missions. He may or may not have found a genie in a bottle on his last mission and eventually married her.

1969: Mario Puzo's novel, *The Godfather*, is released.

March 4, 1972: *The Godfather* premieres. Italian-Americans all agree that it is the greatest movie ever and that to even try to do a sequel would be crazy.

May 15, 1972: Frank Serpico is awarded the NYPD's Medal of Honor for speaking out against police corruption. The movie *Serpico* was made the following year, starring Al Pacino.

1974: *The Godfather II* premieres. Italian-Americans all agree that they were wrong, that *this* is the greatest movie ever and only a moron wouldn't want another sequel.

1976: Joseph Pistone goes undercover as Donnie Brasco, leading to over 200 indictments, 100 convictions, and a $500,000 contract on Pistone. To this day, he travels in disguise under different names and always carries a gun. Don't start this guy's car!

May 17, 1976: Abraham Beame, Mayor of New York City, begins "Italian Culture Week." In 1985, it is moved to October to coincide with Columbus Day. Eventually, it gets expanded to the whole month. Give us a few years, we'll get it expanded to a whole quarter.

November 1976: *Rocky* premieres. The movie is so perfect everyone agrees that there's probably no need for a sequel.

1978: National Italian-American Sports Hall of Fame opens in Chicago. Nice!

October 14, 1978: Pope John Paul II is elected pope and stays pope until his passing in 2005. He's the first non-Italian pope in 455 years. Well, we had a good run.

June 15, 1979: *Rocky II* premieres. Italians prefer the second movie because Rocky actually wins.

1980: Italian wine now makes up 55 percent of the US market. That's up from 18.4 percent 10 years prior. Of course this doesn't count every Italian-American making wine in the garage.

1981: Donkey Kong premieres along with the game's hero, Mario. In those days, Mario worked in construction. He beat that monkey with nothing but a hammer and a mustache.

1982: *Rocky III* is released. The trilogy is complete!

July 12, 1984: Geraldine Ferraro becomes the first woman and first Italian-American nominated to be Vice President in a major US political party.

1985: *Rocky IV* is released. Italians everywhere must remodel their basements so they can fit four framed movie posters.

1988: Brian Anthony Boitano wins a gold medal in Men's Figure Skating for the USA. He also won a ton of championships before and after that. See that? Italians can be graceful, too!

1989: The US government lifts the ban on importing prosciutto from Italy. Finally, Italian chefs got something else to stuff in figs.

1990: *The Godfather III* premieres. Italian-Americans everywhere agree never to speak of it again, and that this is what happens when you let your kids take over the family business.

1990: *Rocky V* released. Italians immediately have something to make them forget about the third Godfather movie.

December 1992: John Gotti goes to prison, ending the reign of the Teflon Don. Gotti is the last of the flashy mobsters from his era, and crime families realize that taunting the cops in the media is no longer possible, no matter how funny it is.

1995: Robert Gallo, Paolo Lusso, and Fiorenza Cocchi publish a major scientific paper that leads to a class of drugs used to treat HIV. Gallo is a major contributor in HIV/AIDS research. He dreams of a day, as we all do, when we can go back to the '70s and just ride bareback all day long.

January 10, 1999: *The Sopranos* premieres. Fans of the show multiply quickly and everyone loves it.

2000: The US government lifts the ban on mortadella and speck, and Italian delis get just that more delicious.

April 28, 2001: Dennis Tito becomes the first tourist in space and his luggage is fuckin' *gone*.

2004: The Order of the Sons of Italy ask Silvio Berlusconi, the prime minister of Italy, *not* to award Robert De Niro honorary citizenship because the actor has "made a career of playing gangsters of Italian descent."

2006: *Rocky Balboa* released. Italians begin to realize that they have raised their kids on Rocky movies. Do we have it great or what?

June 10, 2007: The final episode of *The Sopranos* airs. Confused and angry Italians immediately go back to the watch the first three seasons.

2010: Hammonton, NJ, has the highest percentage of Italian-Americans in the state of New Jersey, according to the US Census: 44.6 percent of the residents. That's why the Italian restaurants there are plentiful and delicious!

2010: Red Dead Redemption video game is released and goes on to sell 11 million units. Italian-American video game maker, Christian Cantamessa, is credited for much of the game's success as its designer.

October 8, 2012: Il Centro, New York's first Italian-American Community Center, opens.

December 20, 2012: *Jersey Shore* finally goes off the air. In the aftermath, Italians must again work to rid the world of the Italian-American stereotypes and The Situation. Local Anti-Snooki laws passed in most Jersey Shore communities.

2013: Most of the bans on other Italian cured meats are lifted by the US government. Originally put in place in the 1960s because of the worry of hoof and mouth disease (and competition), you can now make a cheese and meat plate worthy of an Italian villa!

2015: Fairfield, NJ, becomes the most Italian place in the United States! With 50.3 percent of the people being Italian, you gotta love it. You can't shout "Oh!" without it echoing all over the city!

November 20, 2015: *Creed* released. Jesus Christ, Sly, how many times can I remodel a basement to fit these movie posters?!

August 24, 2016: Central Italy is rocked by an earthquake measuring 6.2. Within hours, Italian-Americans all over the US raise money for the victims of the quake.

March 23, 2017: Representative Zoe Lofgren introduces H.R. 1707, a bill that would officially apologize for the treatment of Italian-Americans during World War II. Better late than never, right?

2018: *Creed II* premiere date. Just start your own fuckin' channel already. Stallone TV. Who wouldn't watch that?

About the Author

Tony DiGerolamo is a New Jersey writer of comedy, movies, books, comics, and games. He is best known for his work on *The Simpsons* and *Bart Simpson* comics. He's been a writer for *Politically Incorrect with Bill Maher*, *Space Ghost: Coast to Coast*, and the Comedy Central website. Tony's screenplays include *The Evil Within* and *Mafioso: The Father, The Son*. He has written novels, including *Fix in Overtime* and *The Undercover Dragon*, and graphic novels, including *Lester Crenshaw Is Dead* and Mark Twain's *Personal Reflections of Joan of Arc*. He is also the creator of *Tony DiGerolamo's Complete Mafia for d20*. His webcomic sites include *Super Frat* at www.superfrat.com and the *Webcomic Factory* at www.webcomicfactory.com.